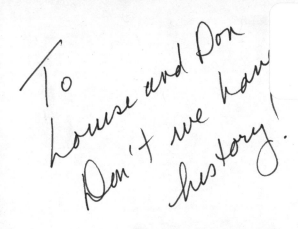

Footsteps of a Woman,
Beautifully Adorned

*A Sister's Journey of Grief, Discovery,
Love, and Understanding*

BY RENE RICKARD

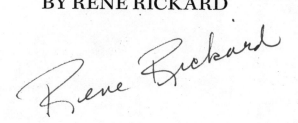

 **FriesenPress**

Suite 300 - 990 Fort St
Victoria, BC, Canada, V8V 3K2
www.friesenpress.com

Copyright © 2015 by Rene Rickard
First Edition — 2015

ISBN
978-1-4602-6187-3 (Hardcover)
978-1-4602-6188-0 (Paperback)
978-1-4602-6189-7 (eBook)

1. Family & Relationships, Death, Grief, Bereavement

Distributed to the trade by The Ingram Book Company

Dedicated
To
Barbara

FORGIVING in her heart
FIRM even when proven wrong
FEMININE to a fault
FERVID for a cause
And
LOVED ferociously.

Acknowledgements

To Sherry, for putting everything on hold, in order to take this life changing journey with me and her Auntie Mame.

To Sherry's family, (Termite and the boys, Vincent and Liam) for taking care of business at home with no complaints, only patience and support during their many weeks without their mom/wife.

To Bob, who held down the fort at home, cared for the four-legged critters and unfailingly dealt with my long convoluted emails.

To Wanchai, who brought food, transported us, fetched, gathered and complied, all the while in his own personal hell as his darling girl slipped away.

To Steve, who translated when needed, made us meals, kept things in order in Doi Saket and without whom many tasks would have been impossible to complete.

To Elizabeth, whose heart was in Chiang Mai with us, always ready with an encouraging response.

To Dean, Robin, Reed and Ruby, my NJ family, who quietly felt our pain and kept it all real.

To the other ever present friends, (you know who you are), who offered rein-
forcement when my own fortitude faltered. The photos were wonderful.

To Barbara's Thai family, who loved and supported her unconditionally.

To the Staffing Office: You wonderful people emailed and told stories, sent
pictures and kept our spirits up. Thank you.

Prologue

MY sister Barbara spoke the words, but they fell on ears closed tight for that message. "Rene, I have pancreatic cancer." I thought perhaps there was a bad phone connection, as Thailand was far away. No line crackle was evident, but these words could not be correct.

"The tests showed a mass on the pancreas. I think they said the tail."

My ears closed tight again. This could not be true. There had been no warning, no "I might have," no "they suspect." Just, "Rene, I have pancreatic cancer."

It was time to make some decisions. I would take this journey with her. I loved her dearly. I was grateful that our mom was no longer alive, as this would have broken her heart instantly; instead, Mom's heart had slowly ceased to work after 89 years.

This story would have been quite different if our original plan of going to Bali for a holiday had actually transpired. A simple shift in destination changed my little sister's life; she went from working and travelling to living mostly in Thailand in as close to ecstasy as she could imagine.

In March of 2006, my sister Barbara and I took a twelve-day tour of Northern Thailand. I left my husband, Bob, at home on Vancouver Island to grudgingly care for the dog; when I had invited Bob to come along, he had declined, envisioning a holiday that consisted of following us in and out of clothing stores. He knew how much we sisters loved our finery. Shopping, however, was not our purpose. We called this trip our "Temple Tour," and during this whirlwind jaunt, we visited *wats* (temples) from Bangkok to Chiang Rai and as much as possible in between.

Instead of the usual crowded touring bus, our transportation consisted of a private van with a driver, Mr. Ot, and an English-speaking guide named Yo. No one else wanted to tour temples in Northern Thailand. Bonus!

Our holiday began at the Rama Gardens Hotel in Bangkok, which had no front doors, so the lobby was open to the outside. Small birds flew in and out as we registered, and we couldn't wait to drag our suitcases to our room, unpack, and then explore the lush grounds. We had never seen a "spirit house" before, so we spent quite some time examining the ornate 6-foot-high structure nestled in the front gardens. Barbara and I were the only people to be seen outside. It was over 100°F that afternoon, but we were oblivious of the heat. We were in Thailand, starting our great adventure!

Later, we asked our guide, Yo, about the spirit houses that seemed to be everywhere. She explained that *Animism,* probably the world's oldest religion, involves the belief that nonhuman entities possess a spirit or soul. Animism became partially entwined with Thai Buddhism. These spirits were usually protective of land, home, and buildings but sometimes could be mischievous. If provided an attractive home or shelter, the spirits wouldn't cause problems for the people who lived or worked in the homes and buildings. Spirit houses could be simple wooden structures (usually mounted on a pillar at eye level) or large, elaborate buildings, complete with images of animals and people. They were in front of almost every home, business, office, or building. We eventually learned that this was a fundamental feature of Thai life.

We visited the King's Summer Home and the ruins of the old capitol of Thailand, Ayutthaya, which was destroyed by the Burmese in 1767. The ruins were sad and spectacular, as were the ruins at Sukhothai Historical Park.

Six days into our trip, after touring dozens of *wats,* many small villages, and several elephant conservatories, we found ourselves in Chiang Mai. Unbeknownst to me, Barbara fell in love with this magical, ancient city. We were there for three days, spending the evenings wandering the night markets and the days doing the usual tourist things. We took in as many Buddhist temples as we could. Several times we rose with the dawn to observe the collection of alms as the villagers fed their monks, who paraded barefoot with their bowls. The practice of giving, being practiced in this manner, was a new concept for Barbara and me.

Neither of us had visited Asia before, but we were open to experiencing a different culture. We were cautioned to drink only bottled water and were warned never to eat street food. We dined only in the recommended hotels, consuming the meals that were part of our tour package. The water issue remained constant, but we learned too late that part of the thrill of travel was to consume the traditional foods, in the traditional manner, which was on the street.

No one warned us, however, about the Thai Toilet, better known as a *squat*. Barbara and I were visiting an ancient *wat* that was inside a mountain. Few tourists ever bothered with this out-of-the-way piece of history. We were amazed and spent quite some time exploring the various rooms inside this cavernous holy place. Then the inevitable happened: We needed to find a bathroom. In Thailand, bathrooms are called "Toilet," usually with an arrow pointing out which direction to take. Our guide brought us to the appropriate area, which consisted of several banks of what looked like outhouses. We were out in the jungle.

Barbara entered one cubicle, and I took another. On the wooden floor was a hole surrounded by a porcelain ring. It appeared to have footprints on each side. There was a bucket and ladle beside it and a water faucet. I stared at it in utter confusion. What on earth was I supposed to do? There was no seat, no raised platform. This thing was flat on the floor!

"Barbara!" I called out.

"What?" she answered.

"I don't know what to do!"

"Neither do I, but I have to go, so I'm going to figure it out!"

There was obviously no help there. I removed my shoes, took off my slacks and underwear, put my shoes back on, and then pretended that I was in the forest, camping back home. There was a use for the water, bucket, and ladle but no toilet paper, so obviously this was a drip-dry situation. I saw a basket in the corner with used tissue in it, but I had no tissue with me. Neither did Barbara. Back to drip-dry. I finally put my clothing back on after rinsing out the "bowl," which was another use for the ladle and bucket of water, and I ventured out of the tiny room to see how Barb was doing.

"Well, that was an experience!" she exclaimed. Our guide, Yo, could not wipe the grin off her face for a very long time. We began to carry tissue with us after that but did not butt heads with a Thai Toilet again on this trip.

Yo loved to torture her two "madams" at times. Once in a park, as we were crossing a leaf-covered area, she quietly said, "Watch out for cobra. They like to hide under leaves." I had never seen Barbara move so fast. Yo thought that was hilarious. She often told us that she was eating "snek soup." Maybe she was.

We watched two funerals taking place side by side at Wat Phra Singh, we played with a baby elephant under the watchful eyes of the mama, we took a long boat ride to Laos, and we crossed the border at Myanmar for a day visit.

We marveled at the signage for the Chiang Mai campus of Buddhist Mahachulalongkornrajavidyalaya University. We were amazed at the vast teak forests, and we observed Buddhist nuns cooking in their humble huts. Our guide taught us how to behave in temples, how to show respect, and how to make merit.

Making merit is part of daily life for Thais, 90 percent of whom are Buddhist. Yo explained that life was about building merit as a result of good deeds, acts, or thoughts. One could feed the hungry, live a moral life, meditate, or be generous to make merit. This merit then carried over throughout subsequent lives. Barbara found all of this fascinating. She had been researching Thai culture and Buddhism for some time. I often realized, when in a temple, that Yo and Barbara were on their knees, in front of a golden Buddha image, while I was still struggling to get my shoes off. It was on this trip that our lives began to subtly move in a new direction.

Both Barbara and I recognized an obvious difference in attitude as we roamed Thailand. Bangkok was the economic center. It was bustling and crowded, with a superior air. The money flow, government, business head offices, large banks, and movers and shakers were in Bangkok. Most tourists thought Thailand was Bangkok, and after taking in the usual sights, tourists then headed for the Phuket area, with its sand beaches and warm waters. We experienced something totally different, and Chiang Mai was at the center.

Centuries ago, Chiang Mai was the capitol of the Kingdom of Lanna, with geographical ties to Burma. The Kingdom slowly disappeared, becoming what was known as Northern Thailand. Northern Thailand was divided into eight provinces, and it was part of the Kingdom of Thailand, ruled from Bangkok. Northern Thailand, culturally Lanna, was where people lived a simpler life. They were farmers and small-business owners. The Lanna ties remained strong in this area, with different cuisine, customs, culture, and music. Architectural evidence of the Lanna influence was everywhere in Chiang Mai in the form of crossed wooden wings on the peaks of buildings.

We were told, "Bangkok struggles with politics, while Chiang Mai watches and laughs." There was a small-city feel to Chiang Mai, even though it housed 1.5 million people. It felt comfortable.

Once back home on Vancouver Island, Barbara could not shake the idea that somehow she was to return to Chiang Mai, even if by herself. It was a frightening thought for her to go without a travelling companion, as she was not well-travelled, but she was determined.

A year later, she had saved up enough money to spend a month in Chiang Mai as a tourist, alone. It was on this trip that she met Wanchai, fell in love, and began her life of bliss. This is her story.

Chapter One

"Go to the edge of the cliff and jump off.
Build your wings on the way down".
—Ray Bradbury

WANCHAI owned a restaurant across the narrow street from the hotel Barbara had booked for her stay in Chiang Mai. After the long flight from Vancouver, she was hungry and tired but glad that after eighteen hours of travel, she was finally ready to relax and perhaps catch a nap as well. It was still morning in Chiang Mai.

As she got out of the taxi and waited for her bags to be extracted, two gentlemen were watching her from the front patio of the restaurant across the way, where they were having coffee. One was Wanchai, a Thai national born and raised in Chiang Mai, who spoke only a few words of English. The other was his bilingual friend, Steve, who hailed from the United States. Wanchai spotted Barbara and was instantly hit with the thunderbolt.

"Steve, go talk to her! Find out if she married or has partner! She the most beautiful woman I ever see!" Now, Barbara was a very attractive lady, but at age 58, she was 17 years his senior — although from a distance, age was irrelevant.

She disappeared into the hotel.

Up in her room, Barb unpacked, sat on the edge of the bed and began to softly cry. What on earth was she doing? She was in a strange country, all alone. She didn't speak the language. She didn't even know where she was! And she was planning to spend a month here? What had she done?

She decided to shower, put on cooler clothing, and walk up the street three blocks and back down the street three blocks. Then she would look for a lunch place. That would be a start.

Once outside, feeling somewhat refreshed, Barb decided to turn to the right to begin a short inspection of her neighbourhood. The narrow paved road was typical of streets in the city, winding, with shop doors nudging the roadside. A closed tavern was kitty-corner to her hotel, and at night it would be bursting with music and the chatter of tourists and Thais.

The restaurant in front of her had a wide frontage with several entrances and a facing patio with wooden tables and chairs. A *chedi* or *stupa* was on the left, in a state of ruin, still wrapped in a saffron cloth, but it was part of the restaurant. *Chedis,* which look somewhat like brick pyramids, have been built for centuries to house relics of honored monks and cannot be deliberately destroyed. Barbara decided to explore the structure later, but fate was about to intervene. She heard English!

"Hello! Welcome to Chiang Mai! Come on over for a cup of coffee!"

The gentleman speaking looked safe enough. It was broad daylight, the veranda was in the open, and the motorbikes zoomed by at a rate of one every 30 seconds, so she sauntered over to the table. The man who had spoken to her introduced himself as Steve. He surreptitiously looked at her ring finger. No wedding ring.

"Are you travelling with your husband?" Steve inquired. "We have great dinner portions for big appetites!"

"No, I'm not married. I'm here to explore Chiang Mai. I'm going down the street for a few blocks and then to look for a lunch place."

"Come back here and have coffee and look at our menu. We have wonderful soups, all made fresh. I can direct you to a few must-sees in the area." Steve was very friendly.

While Barb was chatting, she noticed that the handsome Thai man sitting with him kept staring at her and smiling. It made her feel a little uncomfortable, in a blushing sort of way.

All this sounded good to Barb. She was a bit hungry, and the man called Steve spoke English! Her focus for this trip was to experience Thai culture, not connect with *farangs,* which was what English-speaking tourists were called, but this did look like a nice place to eat.

"I'll stop by on my way back and have some lunch. Thanks." Down the road she strolled, careful to avoid the mosquito-like motorbikes that flew by with reckless abandon, sometimes with just a driver and sometimes with two or three passengers. Thailand! Thailand!

The street — a typical Chiang Mai business thoroughfare with small shops, bars, eateries, and vendors — was very busy, as the locals did their best to eke out a living, usually selling something. She returned in a little over an hour, ready for lunch.

While she was gone, Wanchai was full of questions, for which Steve had few answers, other than that she said she was not married. But she could be in a relationship. Or not interested.

"You find out if she have someone. Please, Steve! She so beautiful!"

Over the years, I have heard this story many times — in Barbara's words, Steve's words, and Wanchai's. Barbara resisted this relationship partly due to the age difference, language barrier, and cultural differences and partly because she had decided to spend the rest of her life working and travelling and then just living and travelling; her plan did not include any kind of personal liaison. She had been on her own for a very long time.

Barbara's nomadic nature caused her to live in many western Canadian cities while raising her two children. She'd had two failed marriages and a handful of failed relationships. She knew she would never marry again. Her children were on their own now.

She laughingly told me once that if she was in a room with one hundred men and one was a loser, she would be on his lap in ten minutes. When she did fall for a regular guy, her relentless jealously quickly stopped the development of anything that might become long term. Finally, she gave up on the idea of growing old with someone of the opposite sex. She was, however, very devoted and successful in her career, and so she became content with her life. Her job as a hospital scheduler was fulfilling, mostly due to the people with whom she worked. She was a hospice volunteer, and her days were very full.

Our mother purchased a large home on Vancouver Island when she moved from Ontario to British Columbia when she was 72 years old. Barbara lived on the lower level, while Mom took over the main floor. It was a good arrangement: Mom didn't have to live alone, and Barbara didn't have to cook. My husband Bob and I lived about twenty minutes away. I loved being close to my mom and my sister after decades of living so far apart.

Barbara had decided that she would live the rest of her life as a single woman doing as she pleased, when she pleased. Someone like Wanchai was not in the cards. Wanchai, however, was relentless. Barbara was to be his, and so began the courtship, with Steve, the intrepid interpreter, always within earshot or poking distance. Steve confided in me that he got very tired of going on Wanchai and Barb's "dates," and he was happy when they took off together, language dictionaries in hand.

Barbara went on many tours, as any good tourist must do, but each day she became more and more involved with Wanchai. She went to markets with him as he purchased the food for the restaurant, and he took pride in showing her his beautiful Chiang Mai. He took her to Mae Sa Waterfall, which cascaded into eleven different pools for swimming. They picnicked and waded in the warm waters while Steve continued to translate each exclamation, question, or answer.

Barbara visited various Chiang Mai hill tribes and was intrigued by their culture. There were seven main tribes: the Karen, who were weavers from Myanmar; the Lahu, farmers from Myanmar; the Lisu from Tibet, who tended livestock; the Akha from Tibet and Myanmar, who were excellent silversmiths; the Hmong from Yunnan, famous for embroidery; the Mien from China, who were embroiderers and silversmiths; and the Padaung from Thailand, better known as the Long Neck Tribe, as many women in the tribe wore brass rings around their necks. The tribes sold their wares as a means of earning money for their families, while the Long Neck Tribe was a curiosity to tourists. Each group had its own customs, language, dress, and spiritual beliefs. They were fascinating!

During their daily travels, Wanchai took Barb to visit dozens of Buddhist temple complexes. As Wanchai introduced her to the beautiful temples in the city, she learned that the grounds contained many buildings, each serving a purpose:

- The largest building was the *wiharn,* or convocation hall, and it was a gathering place for meditation.
- The smaller *bote* was the most sacred building, and often women were forbidden to enter.

- The *chedi* was a place of meditation and symbol of deceased loved ones. It contained relics of monks.
- The monks' quarters were *gooti,* or small huts.
- A *sala* was an open-sided building for ceremonies.
- Some temple grounds had *haws,* or towers, which were small roofed buildings that protected scripture or sacred readings.

Monks were everywhere in Thailand, and most men — including Wanchai — served part of their lives as monks. It might be for several years or only for a few weeks. Buddhism in Thailand was not a religion but a way of life, often described as a philosophy, and more than 90 percent of Thais were Buddhists.

Barb and Wanchai went to the elephant camps, marveling at the clever pachyderms who could gently extract paper money from your hand and pass it up to the *mahout,* or trainer. She took a massage course. They went to the monkey show. They wandered through markets and spent evenings at the restaurant, Wanchai working while Barbara read or visited with farang customers. The month was slipping by too quickly. Steve was the resigned third wheel, although Wanchai's English vocabulary was expanding, and Barb picked up many Thai phrases.

Wanchai had fallen in love the minute he saw her. It took Barbara almost three weeks.

One night after enjoying dinner at the restaurant, Wanchai as usual walked Barbara across the street to her hotel. This time, however, he held her hand. There had been no physical contact between the two of them up until now. Barb told me that a familiar feeling of warmth flowed up her arm, across her chest to her head, and it had been decades since she had experienced this thrill. They said goodnight, and she went up to her room. Now she was confused. Just what exactly did this mean? Wanchai was too young, and she certainly couldn't get involved with someone who lived in a different country. But her stomach was churning, and her head was spinning. Oh, Oh!

Wanchai returned to the restaurant and said to Steve, "She leaving soon. Need do something. Need do something now!" Steve just shook his head.

Wanchai went into the kitchen and prepared a bowl of Barb's favourite soup. He crossed the street, entered the foyer of the hotel, and asked the desk clerk to release the elevator door. The Thai conversation became heated.

"You cannot go into hotel. You not staying here," said the clerk.

"I have soup for lady, floor five. She phone me. She hungry!" Wanchai used his best charm.

"Leave soup here. She can come and get."

"Cannot! Lady want soup now! She hungry! Open elevator door! She good customer! Lose customer if not get soup!" Thais understand good business measures, so the clerk reluctantly released the elevator door, and Wanchai rode the elevator up to floor five. He knocked on the door of Barbara's corner room. He knew it was hers, because he often saw her sitting on her balcony, which overlooked the street and restaurant.

A very surprised Barb opened the door. Wanchai pushed past her into the room. He placed the soup container on the small dining table.

"What is it, Wanchai? What's happened?"

"Bring you soup!"

"I already ate dinner, Wanchai."

"Yes. Need soup, see you." Now Barbara was really confused. They had just spent the evening together. They looked at each other. No one spoke. Then he made his move. The romance was on.

A week later, when Wanchai (and Steve) took Barbara to the airport for her flight back to Canada, Wanchai could not stop crying. "You not come back. Never see you again!" Barbara promised him that she would return. And she did.

While they were physically separated, living in different countries, Wanchai and Barb Skyped each night for a minimum of an hour. Over the Internet, she slowly taught him to speak English, and they slowly learned about each other.

Wanchai told Barbara that his youth was turbulent. He had run away from home, finding solace at the village temple in Doi Saket where his family lived. The monks convinced his parents to allow Wanchai to stay at the temple and to receive the rest of his education with them. He was, however, not destined to be a monk for life. He finally left the monkhood, found a job working as a truck driver, and married a beautiful village girl named Noi. When his son Art was born, Wanchai built a house for his family in Doi Saket, about twenty minutes from Chiang Mai, and tried to be a good husband and father. He was a good father.

Noi and Wanchai separated and began to live their lives apart, but he was adamant that his son be given as many advantages as possible. Art went to private Thai school during the week, and as soon as he was old enough, he attended English school at the YMCA in the city on Saturday and Sunday mornings. Wanchai and Noi shared the responsibility of transporting their son to and from school on the weekends.

Steve and Wanchai had been friends for a very long time, and Steve, who was a retired expat from the States, was encouraging when Wanchai decided to open a restaurant for tourists. It was not far from the Chiang Mai moat that protected the city from invaders centuries ago.

Life took on a gentle pattern for Wanchai. The restaurant had been open for about a year, and it was busy. Art was 8 years old and lived with his mom, and Wanchai was romantically uninvolved. Then he saw Barbara, and everything changed.

If they had met a decade earlier, their relationship would have ended at the airport in Chiang Mai, when Barbara was returning to Canada; phone calls were far too expensive, and Wanchai could not read or write English. But the marvelous Internet now allowed them to use their English/Thai and Thai/English dictionaries to have their conversations, and they spent more time together talking than most adults in committed relationships do. By fall, Barbara had enough money saved so that she could return to Chiang Mai, and she went back ten more times before she moved permanently in May of 2012.

During her commuting years, they built a large home on property that Wanchai owned in the village of Doi Saket. Steve built a small home behind theirs, along with a waterfall and a swimming pool. Art and his mom, Noi, lived a block away, as did Wanchai's sister, Pum. Most of the land in this area was owned and occupied by family. Barbara was accepted as part of this tight-knit group, even though language could be a bit of a problem. However, Art was bilingual, Steve spoke fluent Thai, and Wanchai's English was improving constantly. Pum always managed to find someone to translate when she needed to communicate better with Barbara. They became good friends.

The house was built on barren raw land, but once it was finished, Wanchai began the tropical landscaping. The gardens and yard were his pride and joy, and he was continually adding huge trees, water features, and *salas,* which were roofed gazebos.

In the late afternoon, Barb and Wanchai would zip into Chiang Mai on the motorbike, a short twenty-minute run, and he would open up the restaurant. Sometimes Barb stayed there; sometimes she walked to the moat, shopping along the way. It was always interesting, and she usually chose to go into town rather than stay alone in Doi Saket. She told me that every day was like being on a holiday.

Barbara and Wanchai never married legally, as she refused to do so. In Thailand, a legal marriage involved just signing papers at a civil registry office. There was a traditional marriage ceremony that some Thai couples chose to undergo, with no vows but lots of symbolism; it was not legal. Barbara and Wanchai called each other husband and wife, lived together as such, and felt no need for ceremonies. They were committed to each other.

Their Buddhist temple was just down the street. A neighborhood corner store was a block away. There was a nearby hairdresser who operated out of her home. Small soup places and lunch restaurants were within ten minutes of home by truck or motorbike. With a quick phone call, the massage lady came to the house and the exotic coffee vendor drove into the driveway most mornings.

Barbara finally lived in paradise with her love, and she was happy.

Chapter Two

"The trouble is, you think you have time."
—Gautama Buddha

IN December of 2012, Barbara, Wanchai, and my husband Bob and I holidayed together on Phi Phi Island, a side trip during our month-long visit with Barb and Wanchai. We had always flown directly to Chiang Mai and remained there for our entire holiday, so this side trip to Phi Phi Island showed us a different side of Thailand.

Barbara had to convince Wanchai that this would be a wonderful trip for them and that he would be fine. He was deathly afraid of flying. She held his hand tightly whenever they were in the air. I think he made the trip to please the rest of us, although he did enjoy most of it. He and Bob got along really well.

We flew from Chiang Mai to Phuket and stayed in a classy five-star resort a block from the beach. The swimming water was the warmest we had ever experienced, the sand beaches were clean, and the sun was so warm. The downside was that this was one of the tourist meccas of Thailand, and all of Phuket was overflowing with revelers who were often rude and embarrassing. We looked beyond the tourists and soaked up the scenery, the sand, and the sea.

One evening at dinner, Wanchai ordered a beer and was appalled at the price. He called the waitress over to complain, and he told her that back home in Chiang Mai, the same bottle of beer would cost one-quarter of that price.

She responded, "Then go back to Chiang Mai."

Phuket was strictly a tourist destination, and the prices and service reflected a captive audience. The only Thais here seemed to be resident service workers, as Thais did not holiday in Phuket, and neither Barb nor I enjoyed the antics of the goofy travellers. Wanchai was able to translate for us when needed and do some bargaining on occasion.

After two days, we caught the ferry to Phi Phi Island, which was a trip of several hours. The boat was very crowded, and the sun-worshipping younger people spread out on the decks while the rest of us slapped on wide-brimmed hats and long sleeves and slathered any exposed skin with sunscreen.

We landed at the pier and were enthralled by the beauty of this unspoiled place. There were no cars on the island. Luggage was taken to all the resorts by carts, pulled by employees. The paths were extremely narrow, weaving from side to side and up and down. We were exhausted from walking in the heat, but the strong young men were used to the climate. They cheerfully hauled the carts piled with suitcases over the small hills and in between vendors who were hawking the usual tourist paraphernalia.

We checked into our cabins, which rested on stilts, and after unpacking, we all went to see our resort pool, which was so warm, so clear, so inviting. It was only steps away from the pristine beach, dotted with *long-tail boats,* which were Thai craft of suspect seaworthiness powered by noisy engines with very long propeller shafts that could be raised easily to travel over shallow sand bars. They had a system.

We spent the first day just lazing about the pool and the ocean, stopping this strenuous activity occasionally to have food or a cold drink. We booked a long-tail boat for the next day, so the following morning at 11:00, our driver and his wife pushed the boat into the clear waters. We motored for Pileh Cove, reputed to be the best snorkeling experience in the vicinity.

Wanchai was a strong swimmer, but he showed obvious concern when after twenty minutes, the seams of the hull planking on the boat began spewing water into the wooden ship. Our driver activated the sump pump.

The guys snorkeled for quite some time, but Barb and I stayed on board even though we were wearing swimsuits. The snorkeling would have been fun, but there was no way that either of us could easily climb back into the boat, and we were not prepared to provide the entertainment for the passengers in the other boats in the lagoon.

The forty-five minute trip back to our resort was tranquil despite the roar of the old engine and the heat of the tropical climate. We were under a canopy cover, so sunburn was not an issue.

That evening after dinner, we strolled down the pathways, passed by the noisy hawkers, purchased a few souvenir t-shirts, and soaked up the ambience of this romantic getaway.

The next morning, I awoke at 5:00 when the sun rose, long before anyone else was up. I put on my swimsuit, walked down the path to the beach, and slipped into the warm waters of the Andaman Sea. Glorious! After swimming for a while, I treaded water and looked back toward the beach, which stretched out about a quarter of a mile in either direction. I was alone. There was not one single other person on the beach or in the water. A wave of absolute calm and peace swept over me. This was a brand-new feeling.

Two days later, we packed up and left for Phuket once again via ferry and then returned to our hotel for a last night before flying back to Chiang Mai. We would talk about this wonderful excursion many times, and we were so happy that we had decided to take this side trip. The memory of this mini vacation would serve us well. While enjoying the beach resorts, Barbara had noticed that she had indigestion or stomach pains, usually after eating. I was unaware that Barbara was taking antacids regularly. She put up a brave front.

During our month-long holiday in Thailand, Chiang Mai celebrated the Festival of Lights, or **Loy Krathong.** Barbara had attended this famous observance many times, and she was anxious that we experience it too. It was so exciting! All day long, the Loy Krathong anthem played on the radio and through loudspeakers mounted on vehicles, and there were fabulous parades. At dusk, we purchased several floral baskets, some with bread bases, some with banana tree slices used for a base. Ladies arranged flowers on top of the base, with candles and incense inserted as well. We walked along the Ping River, finally setting the arrangements adrift after lighting the candles and incense. The tradition was that one should place one's misfortunes in the little boats, and they would float away. We all laughed because we could not think of any misfortunes to place in our little floral crafts. Thousands of these **krathongs** floated by us as we wandered along the shore.

Later we watched as thousands of sky lanterns were sent into the heavens. *Sky lanterns* were hot-air balloons made from oiled rice paper on a bamboo frame, about 4 feet high by 2 feet wide, with an opening at the bottom. Inside was a fuel cell that was lit, which caused the balloon to float high up into the sky. Sending off a sky lantern was considered good luck.

Once home that night, Barbara and Wanchai placed several flower arrangements in the small creek that flowed across the front of the property, knowing that the fish in the waterway would nibble on the bread bases. Then we lined the driveway, the road, paths, and any surface such as rails or flowerpots with 500 small candles set in little clay bowls. My job was to light the candles. It took about two hours for them to burn out, and then the next morning my job was to pick up the little empty bowls. Wanchai set off a dozen of our own sky lanterns and then finished off with some fireworks. It was a magical night.

Bob and I left Thailand after a wonderful holiday, going home to celebrate Christmas with our family in Seattle. Back on Vancouver Island, I resumed my normal routines, part of which was e-mailing Barb every morning as soon as I woke up and reading her e-mail from the night before. It was like a daily coffee party, even though we were halfway around the world from each other. We shared our daily occurrences and talked about silly things.

During this time, Barbara spoke lightly of her digestive issues, shrugging off my queries of concern. She didn't want to worry me. She had lived a very healthy lifestyle for decades, eating organic foods, exercising regularly, no drinking or smoking.

In January, Barb's pain came and went. But when it came, it was so debilitating that she was confined to bed, escaping for only ten or fifteen minutes at a time, and she had little energy. She had good days and bad days. Finally she was diagnosed with gastritis, as her stomach was inflamed. Exploratory testing began.

A month later, one of the scans showed gallstones, so Barb's gallbladder was removed. After the successful surgery at McCormick Hospital, she went home, secure in the knowledge that after three months of pain, she could finally get on with her life.

Barbara was re-admitted to hospital within a few weeks, as the pain had not subsided — and it should have. And so began the doctor and hospital visits with twelve different scans and scopes, ending with an MRI. The medical team thought a stone might have migrated out of the gallbladder into a duct, accounting for the almost constant pain. Finally, an in-depth CT scan clearly showed a tumor on the tail and body of the pancreas. More scans revealed affected lymph nodes and spleen and small spots on the liver and the lungs. The tumor had metastasized. It was March 20, 2013.

How could this be? The worst cancer in the worst place! No warning, no real symptoms screaming, "Cancer!" There was just the reality of a horrendous diagnosis. Barbara had invasive cancer of the pancreas.

After examining her medical and lifestyle history, her physicians agreed that the cancer was most likely caused by the fact that Barb had been a smoker from a very early age. She'd stopped smoking seventeen years before her diagnosis, but the cancer cells would have already been growing for three to five years.

This cancer is called "the silent killer," and when mentioned to a physician, it usually causes a reactive shudder. The average pancreatic cancer patient, when the tumor is on the tail or body of the organ, survives only three to five months after diagnosis.

Chapter Three

"Our prime purpose in life is to help others.
And if you can't help them, at least don't hurt them."
—The Dalai Lama

AFTER Barbara's phone call on March 20, 2013, I began to research pancreatic cancer. There was a plethora of information available, most of it not encouraging, and I found myself jumping in and out of denial, looking for a place of comfort that said, "It is not so!" but then falling back into the hole that said, "It is so. Wait for more information." In my conversations with Barbara in my head, I asked, "So now what do I do? How do I comfort you? How do I take some of the burden? How do I accept that this is okay, is part of life, is natural?" These dialogues were one-sided.

I felt utterly helpless, and I couldn't begin to imagine how she or Wanchai felt. Their world was falling apart. But for fate, Barbara and Wanchai would have missed each other. Thailand had become her home and her heart. She was meant to be there, meant to be with Wanchai.

I knew that I would go to her — that was a given — and the course of action would become clearer once we were together. My sister and I would take this journey together: same path, different destinations.

I sat and worried about how this was to be played, and so many thoughts whirled through my consciousness. Strangely, I did not think that the terrible ache would appear so soon.

My dear friend Elizabeth spent that first afternoon with me, and we talked about Barbara, how proud I was of who she was, how lucky I was to love her, how few siblings bring each other joy. She brought me joy. Elizabeth talked about her late husband and their final journey together. John had passed away at home from lung cancer a few short months before. We wept. Elizabeth would be there to support me, just as I had supported her, and she offered to come to Thailand if I asked. Love comes from many different places.

I had questioned so much regarding Mom's death a short year ago, as had Barbara, but Mom gave the gift of Thailand to Barb when she died. With Mom's passing, Barbara was able to move to her home in Chiang Mai permanently. Mom had often encouraged Barb to make the move, but Barb was adamant that she would not leave Canada as long as she had Mom. She had no trouble commuting between Vancouver Island and her home abroad, and her employment was flexible, so her life was one of always either coming or going. Her ties to her Canadian home remained strong.

Our family hadn't given me a lot of experience in coping with death. My first real loss was my grandmother, who died of breast cancer when I was 16. I clearly remember the funeral service, but at that age, my grieving period was relatively short. At 16, life was not about long-term family grief; it was more about what to wear to the dance on Saturday night. The cocoon of youth was sheltering.

Even my father's passing in 1989 in Ontario was buffered — this time by distance. His initial stroke left him tied to a hospital bed for sixteen months. Mom visited him twice a day and took care of his personal needs, taking a four-day break once to visit us on Vancouver Island. Dad thought she had been gone for only a few hours. When I visited him, he did not know me and called me "nursie." It was shocking to think that I was losing my dad, my mentor in so many ways. He was the man who taught me to dance, who encouraged a love of jazz, who would argue with me for hours about nonsensical subjects, teaching me that opinion means nothing; facts and the truth are what count. He was fiercely proud of his family and loved my mother to the depths of his soul. I believed what he told me. His personal integrity was a roadmap for life, even though he struggled with his own demons.

Mom wrote a couple of times a week to keep us updated on Dad's condition, and we phoned occasionally. We were kept abreast of the medical information, but I did not live through the daily vigil of watching a loved one slowly slip away.

My only other close experience with loss was still so recent that I had little perspective. For many years, I had phoned my mom every day and saw her at least twice a week for lunch or coffee, and we volunteered together at an art gallery. She and Barbara lived together. We were all very close. Mom, who had still lived in her large home, did her own gardening, oil painted, and took care of her pets, had started to show signs of heart issues in the spring of 2011. She visited Thailand with Barbara that summer, spent Christmas with her great-grandchildren in our home, and succumbed to congestive heart failure in February of 2012. We were shocked when Mom went to the hospital to balance medications, and she was gone a couple of weeks later.

Bob and I were visiting Wanchai and Barbara in Chiang Mai then, with the blessing of Mom's heart specialist, who had said, "Don't put your life on hold. Eila could carry on for many years just as she is, capable of caring for herself and living a happy life." While in Chiang Mai, Barbara and I talked to Mom daily by phone and to her nursing staff, most of whom Barb knew because she worked at the hospital. When Mom succumbed, my daughter Sherry was with her in the hospital, so Mom died with her granddaughter by her side. It was peaceful and gentle.

But this journey with Barbara would be like nothing I had ever experienced. I knew I had to be with her. I had to try to give her whatever I could. I had no tools for this job. I had no expertise. I only loved her.

After our phone call, Barbara was admitted to the Sriphat Building, part of Suan Dok or Maharaj Nakorn Hospital, which was a teaching hospital and part of the University of Chiang Mai. Its emergency services were considered to be first class. Doctors' and specialists' offices, labs, clinics, testing facilities, and pharmacies were all in the same complex, making it easy for patients to maneuver between doctors and testing.

The barrage of testing began in earnest. The cancer had indeed spread to her spleen, some lymph nodes, and close blood vessels. Once her pain was under control, she would be discharged to her home until the first of April, and the team would decide whether any kind of surgery was viable. They felt that if the tumor was inoperable, they might be able to give her chemotherapy.

While in the hospital with Wanchai, Barbara had a shower and saw herself in the mirror. She sat down on the bed, started to cry, and said, "Oh, Wanchai, I am just bones! I'm so ugly!"

Wanchai said, "I no care about outside look. I no see outside look. I only see your heart, and it is beautiful. So you are only beautiful to me." Barbara held those words close to her in the place that Wanchai saw so clearly.

Chapter Four

"I can have McDonald's, and I don't
have to buy wrinkle cream."
—Barbara

BARBARA and Wanchai left the hospital on March 23, 2013 to do a visa run to Myanmar (Burma), as her year's retirement visa was due for renewal. This was a common practice with expatriates, who had to show that they left the country even if just for a few hours. Passports were stamped upon re-entry, and a new visa date was in play.

Wanchai made a bed in the backseat of the truck so that Barb would be reasonably comfortable for the twelve-hour drive each way. Expats were always careful to keep visas up-to-date, for if not, one could be banned from the country for good. There was very little wiggle room.

After Barb got her new visa, they returned to the hospital, and her surgeon suggested that a proper biopsy was needed in order to proceed with treatment. The medical team continued to work on a pain programme. For three days, Barb and Wanchai were in agony. How could this be happening?

Barb was sent home on the March 27, and Bob and I arrived in Chiang Mai the next day, prepared to spend a month with them. A visa was not required of a traveller as long as the stay was not over 30 days.

We all knew that this next month would be her best month — and also that decisions would have to be made while Barb was still feeling reasonable. Chiang Mai was warm and beautiful. Barbara was welcoming and scared. Wanchai was appreciative and in shock.

The restaurant in Chiang Mai, which had been open all day for years, was now only open for dinner, so Wanchai was available during the day to drive us about and take us to medical appointments, with the odd fun trip thrown in.

Barb had an appointment with the biopsy surgeon at 5:00 p.m. on Friday, the day after we arrived. We all went to Sriphat Hospital, finally getting in to see the doctor at 6:10. The hospital uses a queue system, with all appointments set for 5:00. Everyone showed up and waited for their turn. The atmosphere in the waiting area was typically Thai: people visiting each other and drinking coffee, babies squirming, men telling stories, women keeping the calm. The huge waiting area, which served eight or nine doctors, was air-conditioned, so it was comfortable, but outside the temperature hovered around the 100°F mark.

The surgeon was ready to do the biopsy that night, but we had eaten a light dinner before we came, making surgery out of the question. He moved his morning schedule to begin at 6:00 a.m. instead of 7:00 a.m., so her surgery would be at 6:00. I was amazed at the quick adjustment. Barb was admitted to the hospital, and she and I settled in for our first night. Wanchai and Bob went back to Doi Saket.

We had packed overnight bags, as we suspected her biopsy would take place fairly quickly, so we had all we needed. Once in our room, Barb and I sat outside on our large balcony, enjoying the warm breeze, trying hard not to notice the elephant in the room. There would be lots of time later to pet it, walk it, feed it, and wash it. It would not be going away.

In the morning, when the orderlies arrived to take Barb to surgery, I held her hand, and she said, "Don't be afraid. I'll be fine." Here I'd thought I was covering up my feelings like a pro.

I waited in our room, drinking coffee on the balcony and watching the early morning traffic below. I shared the balcony with a half a dozen pigeons, who were interested in seeking out any crumbs that might be available. There were none until I found a soup cracker in my purse and sprinkled bits of it on the rail. They wouldn't touch the crumbs until I left, so I watched them from the inside with the sliding door closed. Thai pigeons look just like Canadian pigeons.

Shortly after Barb was returned to our room, her surgeon came in to talk to me. The biopsy, which consisted of eight tumor samples, showed that the tumor was inoperable and attached to the stomach. Barb was still asleep, and the surgeon spoke to me about the future. He said that she had between three and five months to live, as was typical for this progression, and that she would spend most of it in hospital unless we made other arrangements. But he was not optimistic about any reprieve from chemotherapy. He did say our oncologist was the best. The reason Barb was at this hospital was because of the outstanding oncology team. I realized that the situation was grave and there might not be a miracle.

A couple of days later, Barb came home from the hospital with a bagful of medications, the most important being morphine. Her pain was mostly in her back. The rest was in our hearts. That night I wrote in my journal:

> I am working hard to go to a place of gratitude.
>
> Grateful that Barb and I found each other in such a connecting loving way.
>
> Grateful that she found Wanchai, almost 8 years ago.
>
> Grateful that Wanchai loved her first.
>
> Grateful that Mom's passing allowed her to move permanently to Thailand in enough time that she could experience bliss.
>
> Grateful that she was surrounded by loving family, (most of whom do not speak English!), who love her unconditionally.
>
> Grateful that she has a good friend in Mitt, who is the head monk at their temple, and who blessed our mom.
>
> Grateful that she and I have had many adventures together, from R-Mystique my dress shop, to Phi Phi Island.
>
> Grateful that we share the love of others.
>
> Grateful that my children adore her.
>
> Grateful that my husband adores her and she adores him.

Grateful that we were financially able to go to her, when she needed us the most.

Grateful that I have reminders of her all over my house and my yard.

Grateful that we will now have some time to remember, to tell stories, to laugh and love together.

This totally beats feeling angry.

The first few days at home at Doi Saket were quiet as we attempted to put together a medication schedule. Barbara had so many pills to take, all at different times. We always had the liquid morphine with us. The dose was not strong, but it would take the pain away quickly.

Although Barbara rested a lot, she was a whirlwind when she had energy, checking out her gardens and directing tasks for all of us. On a typical morning, we would all have coffee together in the *sala* (gazebo) by the road, which was the coolest place on the property. Then Wanchai would water gardens, Barb would rest, the housekeeper would wash floors and sweep the driveway, Bob would tackle whatever task was in need of doing, and I would putter about with Barb's wants.

Barb and I talked constantly, except when she was resting. It was as if she had a mountain of information to impart about her life in Thailand, her dreams, and her ideals. There was no self-pity, no whining, no blame. This was her expiration — just as it was her life — and she was going to control it as much as she could.

Sentences often began with "remember when." We talked about our history as children, our memories of our family summer home, the fun that we both had working in the fashion industry, doing fashion shows and handling difficult customers. The stories were endless.

Sometimes a day would be filled with numerous appointments. On one such day, on the way home, Barb insisted we go to Big C, the closest mall, so she could have McDonald's. It was so funny to watch her enjoying the forbidden treat that she had not tried in decades. "I'm free!" she said. "I can eat McDonald's, and I don't have to buy wrinkle cream."

I was trying to fatten her up. She was so skinny. Her little legs were like sticks, and her ribcage was visible front and back. I had been feeding her a very bland diet of open-faced tomato sandwiches, chicken noodle soup, scrambled eggs, ice cream floats, and smoothies, all at her request. She had one pot and one wok for cooking. She didn't cook, so I was lucky she had that.

Wanchai prepared food, even fried eggs, only in a huge wok. He rarely cooked at home with me there. There were two Thai eateries within a five-minute walk, although he usually took the motorbike to pick up rice, soup, and Thai dishes if we wanted. A grocery store or, rather, family general store was two minutes down the road by foot, and we could buy Magnum ice cream bars, Lay's potato chips, tomatoes (two-and-a-half cents each), toilet paper, or hose parts.

Around 10:00 a.m. each day, Wanchai would leave on the motorbike and return with whatever epicurean delight tickled his fancy that morning. It always included sticky rice, a staple in Northern Thailand. Barb often said that even if Wanchai had eaten several times that day, he always felt that he had not eaten unless he had consumed sticky rice. We would scoop a wad of it with our fingers, roll it into a ball, and pop it into the mouth. Sometimes sticky rice was accompanied with chicken on a stick (so tender) or fresh fish or spareribs, and it always came with fresh raw greens and herbs such as Thai basil. It was delicious, and having been to Thailand several times before, we were familiar with tasty Thai cuisine.

There were several Thai delicacies, however, that never became palatable. One was coloured balls of something on a stick, green, pink, white, or yellow. I never asked what they were but just told Wanchai, "No balls on a stick, okay?"

Neither Bob nor I tried any of the variety of bugs, ants, or eels, and often soup would have strange things floating on top. When I pointed to something like that, Wanchai would say, "You no like. No eat." Wanchai, on the other hand, like most Thais, ate everything with relish. Wanchai's favourite food was a whole fish, barbequed with hot sauces, which he called "fis." His "fis" was delicious, especially with sticky rice.

Barbara had been very fussy about her food, but she loved Thai food, and there was always a huge variety available. She hated the fact that her normal fare was far too spicy for her now, but she was eating a bit. That was important.

The household with its people and animals was always a busy hub of activity. Workers and visitors came and went: the water delivery guy, the massage lady, the coffee man selling steaming latte or cappuccino served in paper cups, all coming and going. Twice a week the ice cream truck pulled into the driveway, and we all enjoyed a chilly indulgence.

One day Bob and I washed Thunder the Devil Puppy, who was Angel Puppy for his bath. Thunder just stood there while we sudsed him down twice. He was about 4 months old and about twice our dog's size but would not get much bigger. He had small feet and was full of energy. Bob walked him several times a day. Thunder liked to eat furniture and so was not allowed in the house.

Thunder was often tied up or in his kennel under cover of the huge carport that housed two trucks, two motorcycles, the washing machine, various drying racks, and a large storage counter. There was still plenty of room to move around in this other outdoor room. Bob bought Thunder some chews that he loved to chomp. Teething puppies were tough, and Barb couldn't do anything with him now.

Dao, a rescue dog, was here too. He was frightened of the puppy who jumped all over him, so he hung out with Koke, the German Shepherd cross Barbara had brought from Canada. The housekeeper was supposed to take the dogs out for toilet duties, but she didn't always make sure that they did the job. I picked up the slack. Keeping the dogs walked was a chore in itself.

Barb and I loved to go into the field next door to feed the white bull some ripe bananas, which he loved. He knew that when either Barb or I ventured into his territory, a big treat was coming. Barbara had named the huge animal "Julie," thinking that he was a gentle female. Wanchai agreed.

One day I was admiring Julie's magnificent form when I realized she had appendages that were unbefitting of a female hanging from her underbelly. "Barbara," I said, "Julie is a bull."

"No, she's a big cow. She's so sweet, and she eats out of my hand. She comes to me whenever I go into the field. Bulls are mean and angry and will chase you. You have to stay away from bulls."

"Barbara, look between her hind legs."

There was a pause while Barbara changed her vantage point to get a better view. "Oh, oh! Julie is a bull! Wanchai, Julie's a bull!"

Wanchai quickly replied, "No, Julie cow. Not bull!"

We pointed out the offending apparatus, and Wanchai said sheepishly, "I no look there before."

As we approached Big Julie with our offerings, three massive water buffalo and their babies stopped grazing, and they began to watch us. They didn't move, they just watched. Barb said, "We might have to make a run for it!" but they just continued to watch. Barbara never did get up the nerve to approach them with some tasty tidbits, because their huge horns looked far too ominous. She often left vegetables in the field for them, always keeping a distance, but their owner handled them easily. The water buffalo belonged to Wanchai's brother and were very well fed and amazingly obedient animals. I never tired of watching them. Sometimes they were just a few feet away on the other side of a wire fence.

Wanchai's sister Pum regularly purchased animals that were going to slaughter and brought them to her pastures behind Barb's house. She fed and cared for them for the rest of their lives. Family members also helped care for the menagerie of creatures whose lives had been spared.

Wanchai often added trees and shrubs to the gardens, and one day a large truck arrived with two beautiful trees in full bloom. He was busy in the morning digging two holes beside the driveway, between the house and the road front *sala.* When I asked him what he was doing, he smiled secretly and said, "You wait. You see."

The trees were Leelawadee *(Plumeria)* trees, blooming with fragrant white flowers. The name means "a woman beautifully adorned," and Wanchai said that he planted them in honour of Barbara. She admired these trees, which had been common since the Queen of Thailand changed the name from Luntom, which meant "sorrow," to Leelawadee about ten years ago.

Barbara began to float the Leelawadee blossoms in water in a wide-brimmed bowl. She placed the bowl on a table just outside our bedroom door, where Bob and I often sat in the swing early in the morning. This act gave her pleasure.

Happiness was a priority in Thai culture, and a stranger would have been hard-pressed to recognize the underlying current of fear and despair that we all worked to hide. We tried not to think about it, tried not to talk about it. We acted happy. At this point we did all our grieving one-on-one. We were not yet able to talk in a group or even as a family about the inevitable. If we didn't talk, it wouldn't happen.

The day came for the visit to the oncologist. The usual queue system was in place. We were number thirteen when we arrived at 10:00 a.m., and we got to see the oncologist at 12:50 p.m. Barb was pretty much toast by then. She had to take morphine and her very strong Tylenol just to make it to the appointment.

Barb and the oncologist decided that they are going to try the new cocktail of chemo, which was very aggressive. She had the most common and deadliest form of pancreatic cancer, and they were trying to buy her some time and improve her quality of life for longer. Sometimes it worked.

On Tuesday we would go to the hospital at 8:00 a.m., they would do the intravenous chemo, I would stay with Barbara all day and night, and then we would go home. The first couple of days would be tough with fatigue, but as the week progressed, it was supposed to get better. She was to receive chemo once a week for three weeks and then have one week off. The course was three months, then a CT scan to see changes, and then, if needed, one more week of chemo.

If it didn't work or if she couldn't tolerate the chemo, they would put her on the old regime, which was less invasive but would only give her a bit more time than if they did nothing. Hopefully.

The oncologist gave Barb a new morphine pill, which would give her twelve-hour relief instead of the three- or four-hour relief from the liquid morphine. She could use that for breakthrough pain, though. This should control the pain more effectively.

After the visit with the oncologist, we went to see their lawyer to do some necessary paperwork and arrange for the lawyer to legally act on Wanchai's behalf. Wanchai had to leave us to go and sit in the truck because he was crying, but meeting the lawyer made Barb feel like she was getting her ducks in a row. This was a very emotional day, especially at the lawyers', as the reality of making some final decisions hit hard.

Then, home we went. Barb was getting tired.

Chapter Five

"Don't ever live life vicariously.
This is your life. Live."
—Lavinia Spalding

DURING the month of April, Barb, Wanchai, Bob, and I stayed home at Doi Saket for the most part, with the odd side trip when Barb felt well enough to go out. She would suddenly say, "I feel good. Let's go!" We would drop everything and jump into the truck. We spent a day at Huay Tung Tao Lake, where we had cold drinks under a *sala* and Barb and Wanchai had massages.

The lake was warm, but we hadn't brought swimsuits, so Bob and I just sat on the soft mats and took in the warmth of the tropics. My thoughts selfishly turned to myself. How was I going to be what Barbara needed? How would I be able to find the answers, provide the strength, guide her when she floundered? Perhaps she wouldn't ever ask for that kind of help and would let me off the hook. What if I made her feel bad instead of lightening her load? How could I keep myself from despairing as I watched my sister slowly disappear?

We went for lunch at The Boat, which was a favourite restaurant with a bakery attached. It was near the University of Chiang Mai, so it catered to students in addition to having a full Thai menu. I especially liked the fact that they would bring a "picture menu" for customers who didn't know what the names of dishes meant.

Wanchai was no help; he delighted in watching us order something, receive food that was nothing like what we had envisioned, and then struggle through a dish so spicy hot that it burned before it hit the mouth. I learned to ask him directly about a dish and demand a straight answer, which he would laughingly give, always accompanied with a shake of his head and an uttering of "Falang, falang!" (Thais have difficulty saying the letter *r* so *farang* became *falang.*) Barbara often said that farangs were in Thailand simply to amuse the Thais.

One day Wanchai brought home chicken noodle soup with ingredients in separate little bags (broth, greens, noodles, and chicken pieces) and made a bowl of soup for Barbara. She started to eat her soup. "Wanchai, what's this?!" she said, holding up a tiny chicken foot with her spoon. He took it from her with a smile and crunched it down with a few bites. Now, that was funny!

We celebrated the Thai New Year, which was in April, by driving around in the afternoon in our air-conditioned truck with the windows closed while happy revelers threw cold water on anything that moved — or didn't move. This celebration, known as Songkran, lasted several days, and if you ventured into the city, the only time you'd be safe was in a closed vehicle. We drove around the moat, but the revelers couldn't be bothered with us, as we were in an enclosed truck.

It was 95 to 100°F outside, and people went downtown just to get wet. People rode in the back of pickup trucks just to get wet. They also had barrels of water in the trucks so they could throw water at the people on the sides of the streets. They gave as much as they got. Monks got it, police got it, and tourists got it, but the revelers respectfully left street vendors alone and didn't throw water into the shops. They threw water into the back of red truck taxis, and tuk-tuks had their tops off so their passengers were more exposed. Tuk-tuk drivers hated it, as their passengers had no defense (or they loved it for the same reason). Water guns and hoses were used, while some people had tubs of water on the roadside.

Huge blocks of ice were sold everywhere, so the water in the barrels was often ice water. Barb said she was hit once with ice water and it was so awful she chose to stay away from the celebrations. People took water from the moat or from the river, from everywhere, and the government also supplied ice. All along the moat they sold ice, buckets, water blasters, water backpacks, hats, and of course food and drink. All of the moat area was alcohol-free with huge signs saying "No alcohol," but I think a few imbibed. Lots of vendors supplied drinks to their favourite customers.

We knew that the park was safe from the deluge, so we headed there, and once inside the park area, three of us had a two-hour massage. Massage helped Barbara greatly, relaxing muscles that were usually tense with pain or memory of pain. Massage to Thais was as necessary as personal hygiene, and Barbara had grown to enjoy and depend on it. She always felt better after a massage. There were only three massage slots available, so Bob bowed out and slept on a rented mat on the grass.

I was so glad that we went into the city so we could experience Songkran firsthand. I'd had no idea in advance of what this Thai celebration entailed.

That evening Wanchai had to do his rent collections, so he went into town on the motorbike, taking back roads and alleys. He arrived home dry.

During the month, Barbara and I often went for doctors' appointments, just the two of us. We would hire our tuk-tuk driver, Num, for a half a day or however much time we thought we needed, and I would load Barb up with morphine. We'd climb into Num's noisy beast and rattle into town. It was always an adventure. We both loved to ride in Num's tuk-tuk.

Sometimes we needed to get a few groceries, or dog food, or drug store items, or money from an ATM, and I would be the gofer while Barb rested in the tuk-tuk. At times she felt well enough to join me, and sometimes we would stop for tea or a snack. These trips were so enjoyable for both of us. We laughed with each other, sharing the joy of exploring a new culture, pointing out the ever-present monks, who were often barefoot but talking on cell phones. We found the monks enchanting.

In Thailand, restrooms were labeled "Toilet" except for the ones that were labeled "Happy Place." We giggled at the store named "Happy Mattress." There was "Happy House" (a hotel) and "Happy Green" (a restaurant). Pointing out "Happy" establishments could be a full-time job.

Bob often went into the city with Wanchai when he went to work and would explore the area around the restaurant, telling me later of his finds. After dinner, Barb and I would spend time in the pool or watch reruns of *Nurse Jackie,* which came on at 6:00 p.m. We both looked forward to watching that show. I would make tea and make sure Barb took her medications, and she would talk and talk and talk. I learned to listen intently as she told me of her Thailand, her home, her Wanchai.

Every morning at about 7:15, the speakers down the road made the morning announcements for the farmers, who were all up by 4:00 or 5:00 a.m. Wanchai's brother-in-law had already taken his five truckloads of water buffalo (three to a load) to the pasture for the day. At 5:00 p.m. he would bring them all back, and we sometimes watched these huge, beautiful beasts gingerly back off the ramp on the back of the truck. The babies came off forward. They were very, very expensive. They spent the nights in wall-less barns on the property next door, owned by the family. Neither Barb nor I ever tired of watching these majestic animals.

Each day as the sun came up, the roosters inevitably began their morning serenade, but the rest of the household lay deep in sleep. My resident geckos scurried across the walls, trilling to each other as they prepared for a day of hiding behind pictures, the air-conditioner, and the wall-hung TV.

Ah, Thailand, Thailand!

First chemo was coming up fast. It would be a tough week; the first round of chemo tends to be the worst one, with the body getting hit so hard. Apparently, it would be easier each time — at least in a perfect world.

According to her oncologist, Barb's prognosis was better than we had expected, provided she could tolerate the chemo. It would double her life expectancy if successful, but Barb had made it very clear that she didn't want to know how long she had. A popular TV host, a heart surgeon, said he doesn't do timelines like this because patients have a tendency to obey doctors' orders. I've always maintained that Gramma didn't know she was supposed to die in 6 months, so she lived for another four years.

Barb's spirits were good for the most part. I, on the other hand, became horribly emotional at times, trying hard to keep my feelings from Barb. We both cried in solitude. Wanchai was visible in his agony, while Bob simply disappeared. Each of us dealt with grief in his or her own way. That would change one day.

The night before "chemo day," Barb was in terrible pain, and nothing would help. Wanchai took her to the emergency room. After X-rays, they removed more than 2 feet of compacted feces. No wonder she hurt! She had just recovered from that invasion when the cancer pain kicked in with a vengeance. They set up a morphine drip so she could have a restful night, and Wanchai stayed with her. She was scheduled to start chemo the next morning, so they put a port into her tummy to receive the drugs.

I was supposed to be with her, but I had a terrible cough and so didn't dare go to the hospital. I needed to be able to care for her once she came home.

Barbara's first chemotherapy session was a disappointment. Barb wasn't well enough to endure the very aggressive Folfirinox, so she had to take the more benign Gemcitabine.

The first day at home after the treatment, Barb had lots of energy, and we thought she would be okay. She actually felt good as long as she took her pain medications. Wanchai had some music playing on the stereo one morning, and when *La Bamba* came on, Bob and I danced all over the living room, just the two of us, lost in a moment.

That night Barbara had some flu-like symptoms, the first response to the chemo other than the fatigue that came and went. Wanchai was in the pool, and Bob and I were in bed watching TV. She burst into our room, flung back the covers, and climbed into bed with us. I wrapped my arms around her as she huddled like a small child. My heart was breaking.

I still needed to pack one suitcase filled with memorabilia that had to return to Canada, and we hoped to "do something," as Barb liked to say, before the week was over and I had to go home.

But the next day proved to be the beginning of nasty chemo side effects. She got it all and had no appetite, no matter what temptations I put out there. The doctor told her, "Eat anything! Take in as many calories as you can." But she ate little, and what she did get down came back up.

Wanchai went to her favourite restaurants and brought home dishes that he knew she would enjoy, but they sat in the fridge until I threw them out, or Bob and I ate them. The evenings changed as well, as when Bob went to the restaurant with Wanchai, Barb was confined to her bed. We would still talk or watch television, but she was too exhausted to move about the house or yard. She drank ginger ale and water but couldn't eat. I delivered copious back rubs. At least then I felt useful.

Once Wanchai and Bob came home, I would leave her bedroom. Bob and I would watch a bit of television before going to sleep. We had a new baby gecko living with us in our bedroom; the little guy took longer to find a place to hide. Cute.

Barb and I did get some important paperwork done. It was mostly informing agencies and gathering information for her income taxes. I completed the 2012 taxes, and there was no hurry with 2013. There was no estate.

During this time, Koke, Barb's dog, got tick fever. One morning Wanchai and Koke were playing ball in the living room as usual when the Shepherd cross had a seizure. She'd exhibited no symptoms until then. As sick as Barbara was, she got dressed, and she and I rode to the clinic with Koke resting on blankets and pillows in the truck bed. Wanchai and Bob carried Koke in and put her in an examination room. This was a 24-hour veterinary clinic with a doctor always on duty.

Koke had two more seizures after we left her at the clinic, and she couldn't get up. Wanchai said her eyes were hollow. Seizures were not painful, apparently, and the vet managed to keep her temperature down and keep her comfortable. Being an elderly dog, she couldn't fight off this infection. Thais do not believe in euthanasia for animals (it's bad karma), so we didn't know how this was going to go. Wanchai was so upset, as Koke had become his dog. Barbara would not speak of Koke's probable passing, but her expression spoke volumes.

Koke came home with medication but could only raise her head. Wanchai carried her outside for bathroom duties, which she performed immediately when he set her on her legs, but she did not eat or drink much. He had to bring her back to the clinic after a few days. She remained there until she passed away.

After her second chemo treatment, Barbara did not get the day of reprieve. Straight home and straight to bed she went. She dressed most mornings and took the odd venture out into her gardens, but for the most part was prone in bed, pillows around and beneath her in an attempt to alleviate the discomfort in whatever manner worked for a few minutes. She just felt so bad. I think that Barb was a bit depressed because we were leaving in two days.

Wanchai kept saying, "Why you not stay one year?"

It was going to be so hard to leave her, but there wasn't much for me to do now. Our daughter Sherry e-mailed regularly while we were in Thailand with Barbara and Wanchai. Sherry loved her aunt deeply, and being a paramedic, she had watched families suffer as loved ones succumbed to the inevitable. But this was different; this was close.

Sher asked all the questions that I only thought. Why her? Why now? How can I help? Sherry shared her thoughts and some elementary truths that she and I had kicked around over the years. Sherry's e-mail read as follows:

It is simple I guess,

We are born, we live and we die.

Love people not things!

Do what you dream of, so you don't have regrets.

Find peace in the little things.

Meditate.

Be kind.

I wish Auntie less pain, less fatigue, rest with purpose, have calm slow days of love and life. Experience laughter, not fear.

We will all eventually be okay, we will miss her so deeply, and wish that she were here after she is gone but she will be with us in our memories and in our heads and hearts.

We will make it through this and I hope she knows the depths that she has touched our lives and does every day. I adore my Auntie.

Remember hanging out and playing with the dog, the day we all got stung by bees? Remember all the costumes at the dress shop? Remember Auntie living in the basement on the Lake? Remember all the talks and the teas and coffee parties?

I do!!

Everything will happen and nothing we do will really change it much (at least not the way we would like to change it). I hope this chemo will stop progression and extend her life.

This journey may be long, I hope for that. I hope it is a calm one.

If we lose Auntie earlier, it will seem like such a wrong. I will just keep sending all my positive energy to her.

Mom, there is nothing I can say that you and Auntie don't know or haven't discussed already. You will to cry together and I know you both know that each other understands. I'm sure if you said nothing to one another it would all still be okay.

I hate this! But I try to let that thought move through me and turn to all the love, as soon as that feeling crosses my mind.

I am holding onto you and give one big huge embrace for my darling Auntie. I wish I could take it all away. I wish I could make it better! It sucks being helpless. So we will concentrate on love, kindness, and support.

Love, Sherry

On our last day in Chiang Mai, we went to see the lawyer at 10:00 a.m. and then came home for the day. Barb shared some stories about Wanchai and Thailand when she was feeling up to it. Their life together had been very busy.

In the past, they often jumped on the motorbike and went off into the hills to explore the countryside. She took a photograph of the first and only "wild elephant" she ever saw. Elephants were usually in captivity, either working or in special rescue camps, and the plight of the working Thai elephant became a passion of hers.

On a previous trip, Barbara, Bob, and I spent a day at the Elephant Nature Park, where we watched the herd interacting and swimming in the river, and we fed them and washed them. She and Mom visited the same rescue park for a day, and Barb also went once on her own. It was a special place, a place to be in the wild with these magnificent creatures and to put one's own life into perspective. Of course, some rescued animals weren't considered to be safe around people because these creatures had been so badly mistreated or were in pain. They were kept in separate areas. Spending a day at the camp was a wonderful excursion unlike any other activity. We often talked about the possibility of going again when Barb was well enough.

Before Barbara became ill, Barb and Wanchai did many tourist things, such as rafting down rivers and exploring Chiang Mai's nooks and crannies. Every day was a new adventure for these two people deeply committed to their relationship, gleaning as much happiness as they could out of each day.

It was these memories that often kept that wonderful human phenomenon — *hope* — alive, and they kept Barb struggling for a future, no matter how short.

We talked about these adventures as Barb went through closets and cupboards. So many things that she had brought to Thailand over the years now needed to find their way back to their origin. She directed, and I packed. There would be no cleaning out after the fact, and we both knew this. This, the first of many finalities, hit us hard.

Wanchai and Bob bought identical straw fedoras one day, and the men walked around calling themselves "brothas from anotha motha." A tight bond was forming between them. It made Barbara very happy, as she did not want Wanchai to lose his Canadian family.

I hated the thought of leaving Barbara, but it was time for me to recharge and get ready for the next phase, which I knew would be difficult. Bob and I left Thailand on April 26 at midnight. It was heartbreaking to watch Barbara and Bob hugging each other for the last time. They both knew that this was goodbye. I would be coming back, but Bob would not.

She asked, "How do you say goodbye forever?"

Bob could not get into the truck for a few minutes. He was crying hard. As Wanchai pulled the truck out of the driveway, I looked back at my sister, standing under a Leelawadee, her home and gardens framing her now-tiny body.

I hoped that things would not go awry and take her life before I could return.

Chapter Six

"You sometimes think you want to disappear,
but all you really want is to be found."
—Gautama Buddha

I spent the month of May at home on Vancouver Island. I rested, I gardened, and I tried to mentally prepare myself for the next trip to Chiang Mai. Barbara was unable to e-mail, but she phoned, and we talked for a short time about once a week.

She was always so exhausted that it was difficult for her to read her e-mails, never mind answer them. Her support family began putting prepared food into the fridge so she could just eat, and that seemed to be working better.

She was in a holding pattern, but she was very ill. Getting through the chemo and trying to not lose too much weight was her focus. It was still hot in Thailand and would be for another month, until the cooling showers began, but the gardens were in bloom and so beautiful. She loved her gardens.

I knew that once I went back to Thailand, I would be gone for a long time, so I tried to prepare things at home for Bob. He would be alone, except for the dog and the cat. Little did we know that he would also inherit his grandsons for a couple of weeks. He wouldn't be as lonely as we thought he might be.

Barb didn't receive her next chemo session, because her blood counts weren't high enough. In total, she received only three chemo treatments; she wasn't strong enough to tolerate more than that.

Near the end of May, I received an e-mail from Wanchai's friend Steve. Wanchai spoke very good English now but didn't read or write it. He spoke, read, and wrote Thai, Lanna, and Pali, the language of the temples. That made Steve once again the communicator, as e-mail was our communication vehicle. The e-mail read as follows:

> Dear Rene,
>
> Barbara asked me to ask you to come now. She just can't eat and is really fading fast. I think you should be here too. She is so thin and weak.
>
> Let us know when.
>
> Love, Steve

I had been home less than a month and hoped that I would be able to spend the summer in my gardens. This was not to be. I let Steve know that I was coming as quickly as possible. First I had to go to the Thai consulate to get a visa extension because I knew that I would be more than 30 days, regardless of what happened. I could always fly home earlier if I wanted to do so.

Sherry, our daughter, who lived near Seattle, decided to come with me for a month (no visa required), so I made reservations for the two of us. She had never been to Thailand, and she knew that she could be of great help with her medical background. That made me happy. Sherry and I had always been very close, even though she and her family lived many hours away, near Seattle. We talked almost daily, and she and her children had spent summers with us since they were born.

Our son Dean and his family lived in New Jersey, and they were upset that there was no way for them to assist. Their work schedules were not flexible, and the children weren't old enough to care for themselves, even for short periods of time. E-mailing information back and forth would have to suffice. They would offer their support from afar.

Sherry's neighbors and friends would help with her boys, picking them up from school, and her husband could take some time off work when needed. So many people pitched in so that Sherry and I could fly to my sister's side.

I had this terrible fear Barb's death might happen fast. In the very first phone call that Barbara made to me, way back in March, she had said, "Rene, you have to understand that this could go very quickly, so be prepared for that." She was at that point very realistic. That changed, of course.

Sherry arrived on Vancouver Island on Sunday, and we flew out on Monday. It's amazing how quickly a person can get things together.

The flight was Vancouver to Seoul, with a short connection to Chiang Mai. Sherry and I hadn't slept well prior to leaving (too much to do, too much to worry about), so by the time we boarded the first plane, we were already sleep-deprived.

On the second-leg flight from Seoul to Chiang Mai, I was so tired and tried to sleep sitting up to no avail. The Thai gentleman in the window seat beside me asked the stewardess to seek out a single seat elsewhere for him, and as he left, he said to me, "Lie down. Sleep." Only in Thailand! I slept with my head in my daughter's lap.

We arrived at Chiang Mai International Airport late Tuesday night. Wanchai and Steve were there to pick us up. They were so happy to see us, or perhaps relieved. My wise daughter-in-law once said to me, "Birthing and dying are women's work." These two fine men were very ready to pass on the baton.

When we stopped at a 7-Eleven on the way home from the airport so that Wanchai could pay the electrical bill, we bumped into a friend travelling by motorbike on his way to Steve's in the pouring rain. He was soaked but not cold, so we lent him an umbrella. Off he scooted in the downpour, umbrella overhead, his jacket flapping in the wind, a strange but common sight in Thailand. Gasoline was very expensive in Thailand, so most people had a motorbike, even if they had a car or truck. I laughed the first time I saw an older gentleman driving down the highway on what was probably his wife's pink motorbike. Such things do not bother Thais. They are a practical people.

We arrived at the house in Doi Saket and found Barb resting in bed, tired-looking but not as bad as a few days before, according to Steve. She had brushed her hair and put on lipstick. I wasn't surprised. Very few people had ever seen Barbara without make-up. Wanchai had, of course, and he knew it took some time for her to get herself ready whenever they were going out. About an hour before they needed to leave, he would say, "Time to decolate [decorate], Bahbella! Have one hour!" It worked well for them. Barb and I used that phrase when we needed to fix our hair and put on some make-up. It was fun to say, "Time to decorate! We leave in an hour!"

We loved the interesting translations of English words, always so practical. For example, Wanchai's socks were "foot covers." Whenever Wanchai did or said something that made Barbara upset, he would gently say to her, "Oh, Bahbella, you so beautiful!" She found it hard to stay angry with him.

As soon as Barb saw Sherry and me, she said, "Now I can go to sleep." And she did.

We talked for a short time with Wanchai and Steve, and then Sherry and I unpacked until 2:00 a.m. I gave Steve the lotus flower painting I had done for him. Thunder and Dao were now outside in Steve's yard instead of in the house.

The roosters woke us up at 6:00 a.m. Always, in Doi Saket, the roosters would start my day, letting the world know that the sun was rising and it was time to be grateful that we had once again woken up. Many people hadn't.

We had to leave by 8:30 for Barb's possible chemo session at Sriphat Hospital, so lack of sleep didn't matter. Sherry and I were running on adrenaline, anyway. I wasn't sure what Barbara was running on.

We girls were dropped off at the front door of the hospital, while Wanchai parked the truck. Wheelchairs were lined up at the entrance, so we plunked Barbara into one and headed for the elevator, which would take us up to the thirteenth floor for her blood work.

The huge waiting room was full as usual. After about an hour, we were called up to meet with the oncologist, who had checked Barb's work-up. He said her counts were borderline, but she was far too weak for chemo.

Instead she was admitted to hospital for a nourishment IV, because she was throwing up everything, including medication. The oncologist also ordered a chest patch of an opiate derivative, which had fewer side effects than morphine. This was a new direction.

Admitting Barb didn't take long, and a young porter took us up to the assigned room in the hospital. I stayed with her while Sherry went home with Wanchai to pack a couple of bags for our stay. We didn't know how long we would be here. Wanchai brought back chicken soup and spicy chicken wraps for dinner, and then he went to work. Barbara was hooked up to an IV that delivered a cocktail of various vitamins and minerals, milky white in colour, and that was her dinner. Sherry and I ate the chicken and soup.

Our hospital room was so very different from what we were used to in America. The balcony, a nice size, easily could hold many chairs, and it overlooked large trees and greenery as well as the city. The staff wheeled in a daybed for Sherry, while I would sleep on the comfortable leather couch. We had a full-size refrigerator with a freezer, and the microwave sat on a counter beside it. A flat-screen television faced the sleeping and sitting arrangements. Barb's hospital bed was in the center, for easy access by all. A small dining table with chairs was on the same wall as the fridge, microwave, and closet, and there was still so much room. There were paintings on the walls and draperies on the sliding doors and windows. It was very comfortable.

We hung up our clothes in the wardrobe and filled the drawers with various bits, leaving some shelves and drawers empty. I was asleep by 8:00 p.m., but Sherry and Barb talked until 11:00. They were so happy to see each other.

Sherry and I awoke at 4:00 a.m. and tried to stay quiet, but we ended up waking Barb up too. She had a great morning; she felt better, with no nausea or vomiting. Pain was in her upper and lower back. The upper pain was her cancer, but the lower was from the very hard hospital bed. She phoned Wanchai and asked him to bring her feather mattress from home, which he did, making a huge difference in her sleep comfort.

Sriphat Hospital was part of a very large complex made up of many buildings. The street that housed the hospital and grounds had retail stores and foodies on the other side, so we could get snacks or food very quickly. Sherry was sent across the street to the bakery beside the 7-Eleven to pick up breakfast (rice and eggs). She started by walking down the fourteen flights, and as she entered the lobby, she was astounded by her first impression.

The main lobby was not air-conditioned, as it was open to the outside, with no doors. All along the windows were dozens of gurneys lined up in rows, each with a patient waiting for attention. Crisply uniformed nurses continually moved people in and out of examining rooms. It looked confusing, but she soon realized it was like a well-run bee-hive. The most surprising revelation was that several monks were on gurneys, surrounded by other monks. Somehow it seemed inappropriate that monks were not exempt from illness. Their bright saffron robes stood out amongst the darker clothing of other patients and contrasted with the white garb of the medical staff. Sherry almost forgot to go and get our breakfast. She had worked as a paramedic in New York City, so she was used to a frantic hospital atmosphere, but this was not familiar at all. She could happily have spent the day observing.

Sherry lost her way only once during her excursions for food, when she entered the hospital from the wrong door and ended up in a different building. She found her way back to the bakery and started again, this time managing the correct doorway, and she passed by the landmark escalator that was in the lobby of our building. Walking the stairs each day up and down gave her exercise; she used the elevators only if she needed to hurry. I walked up and down six flights almost daily, going nowhere, just to keep the muscles moving. This became our mantra: *Keep it moving.*

The hospital could have provided food for us from a farang menu, but it was recommended that we bring in our own food. My idea of lunch was not a cheese sandwich on white bread. Wanchai owned a restaurant, so he brought dinners for us, which were always excellent.

Days were very busy, as we were unfamiliar with the hospital routines, and people came in and out constantly. Barb was tough, but she broke down with me, holding me tight when Sherry was out scoring food. Barb didn't do this in the presence of Sherry, on whom she relied for most medical and bedside care. It was rough and would get rougher, I knew.

Barbara's roles were very specific. For Wanchai, she needed to be strong and consoling. For nurses and doctors, she needed to be brave. For Sherry, she needed to be Auntie Barb, fun-loving and adventurous. For me, she was just Barbara, my sister, dying of pancreatic cancer. She kept saying to me, "What would I do without you here?" It broke my heart.

No wonder Wanchai couldn't handle doing this alone! He lived in the now and worried about the future.

Part of her medicine was steroids for inflammation, and she was so hot on the steroids that we had to keep the room like an icebox. Sherry and I wore sweaters and wrapped up in blankets. When we could no longer stand the cold temperature, we took turns out on the balcony, where it was always over 90°F. We didn't leave Barb alone.

The worst part for Sherry and me was the constant feeling of helplessness. To compensate, we hovered and worked on scheduling. I began to journal daily, and I e-mailed Bob, friends, and family as well. This became my grounding and my connection with reality. The iPad was my friend.

Sherry had her iPad as well, so she kept in touch with her husband and her boys, the downside being that we had to leave the room in order to e-mail. The router was down the hall, so we took turns sitting on the floor near the router, jabbing at the screen, always hoping that someone would send us a message.

Barb's white nutrient drip bag took twenty-four hours to empty and was changed each afternoon. The side effects of morphine were constipation, nausea, vomiting, and no appetite, and Barb had them all in spades. Her treatment was all about experimentation, as each patient was different, each cancer was different. And just when things were cooking, it all changed again, causing a new plan of action. We knew who the real boss was: the big C.

For the first time, Barbara said, "I want to die." Her pain was difficult to control and ever-changing. It was heartbreaking. Sher and I were her caregivers, her advocates, and our entire focus was on keeping her pain as low as possible. Palliative care was a possibility, but when and where? Was Barbara ready for palliative care?

I hated my inexperience. I hated the constant heaviness in my chest. I hated the unknown timeline. I loved her.

I wondered how long she could hold on like this. Yet we laughed and reminisced and had much quality time. We were living at the hospital, we were eating out of the 7-Eleven and the little bakery that sold rice and eggs, and we were washing out our underwear. Wanchai brought us our dinners. It was what it was.

At 7:00 p.m. one evening, Wanchai picked up Sherry from the hospital to take her to a concert at his restaurant. She helped serve beverages and enjoyed the concert, coming back to the hospital at 1:00 in the morning with Wanchai and his son Art. They were very excited about the concert and had many stories to tell; they finally left at 1:30 in the morning. Barbara and I had been sleeping, but we were able to wake up and enjoy the chatter. That night, Sherry experienced her first motorbike ride without a helmet and her first time with three on a bike. Interesting how one would never even think of riding a bike in that manner at home, over and above the legal issues, but in Thailand it seemed normal. Traffic was slow-moving and light, and the restaurant wasn't that far from the hospital.

On the first of June, we were up at 6:00 a.m. This was a better day, as Barb finally had a bowel movement. Something we had once taken for granted was reason for jubilation. Hurrah! Everyone had been so worried, as it had been almost two weeks. Life had become about what Barb put in and what came out.

The next day started with a bang. Barb bolted out of bed at 5:00 a.m. with the runs. The bed was fine, and she missed most of the floor, but her clothing and her legs got it. She charged into the bathroom, where Sherry and I stripped her down in the shower. Our bathroom was very large, and the huge shower had no walls, so it was big enough for the three of us. After her shower, Sherry dressed Barb while I cleaned the floor with disinfectant; then the cleaning staff came in and washed the floor well. A nurse unhooked the IV so Barb could don a new top, and we poured Barbara back into bed. After the thorough cleaning, she was exhausted and went right back to sleep. Her blood pressure stabilized.

Sherry massaged Barb's back and feet. Massage was one of Sherry's daily tasks, doing as much as she could many times a day. It helped relieve the constant back pain that Barb suffered.

I was feeling tired, and I shouldn't have been. We needed a new set of bedding for all of us, and Sher scored bedding like a thief in the night. We preferred to do our own changes, but sometimes the bedding cart was skimpy or already out of sight.

Wanchai arrived with a group of young girls who had "vitamins" to cure cancer. Sherry and I walked over to the 7-Eleven, and we strolled around the hospital. When we arrived back at the room, they were all still there, finally leaving after selling Wanchai a bottle of "vitamins" from an MLM company based in Bangkok, worth $17 Canadian. This was very expensive by Thai standards.

There were enough capsules in a bottle for one week. Wanchai was desperate for something that would make this all go away. He was going to cure his darling and get their life back.

Chapter Seven

"There is no path to happiness.
Happiness is the path."
—Gautama Buddha

WHEN the pain doctor arrived in the late afternoon, Barb was very alert and interacted well. He raised her patch strength and discussed a bone scan, as her body was aching all over, and he thought that the cancer probably had moved to her bones. Sherry talked to the doctor outside the room, and he said that Barb had one month or so left, based on her lack of food intake and her pain level. He wanted Sherry to stay longer than the three weeks she had left. The oncologist had been away for a few days, and he would be shocked at Barb's condition.

We all had a nap, including Wanchai. He often climbed onto the bed with Barbara, and the two of them slept, arms around each other. Sherry and I usually left the room when Wanchai came, at least for a while, so that they would have time together alone. They usually just slept in each other's arms. Wanchai was not getting much sleep at home, but he could fall asleep quickly beside Barbara.

That evening, Sherry went to the Sunday Walking Market with Wanchai, so I was alone with Barb after a very tiring day. We talked for a while, but she was not connecting.

Sherry came back to our hospital home at 11:00 p.m., and the nurse brought in Barb's medication. We talked a bit, and then Barb went back to sleep. In the morning Sherry went to the store for our usual rice and eggs and picked up some Pad Thai. When the gastric doctor came in, he saw the Pad Thai on the counter and told us not to eat that tasty dish, as it was bad for the heart. We didn't listen to his advice. Pad Thai was too good to pass up.

At 10:00 in the morning, after waterproofing Barbara's patch and her IV, we gave her a shower as she sat in a plastic chair. We washed her hair. All three of us were in the shower, each with a chore, Barb's being to sit still and behave. This process took a long time and was so tiring for her, but she did feel better, and we felt needed.

At noon, we phoned Steve to order from the restaurant — two tomato soups, two potato soups, two chicken dinners with home fries, and some chicken broth with rice, in case Barb would eat something. Wanchai would bring the food when he came that night.

I looked at Barb's IV port and asked Sherry to check it. It was inflamed after only a few days. The nourishment IV required a fairly large needle, so it easily got irritated with movement. The nurse put in a new port that blew in less than a day, so Barb's pain doctor, who was also an anesthesiologist, put a port in the other arm after using a topical freezing.

Her veins were beginning to look inflamed, like there might be trouble on the horizon. She did not have veins conducive to accepting ports for injections. They were very deep and hard to find, and if a nurse had to change a port, it was poke, poke, poke. Barb began to dread having a port changed. The pain doctor would use a topical first to prevent pain, and he seemed to be able to find a vein when no one else could.

Barb gave some executive orders, saying, "Only my pain doctor is to put in a new port." That worked.

Then she decided that she didn't want to sleep in the hospital bed but would rather have a facsimile of her home bed, which was flat with no adjustments. This was a psychological reaction, I thought, as she associated home with wellness. I talked to her about the fact that she wouldn't be able to adjust the bed, but she didn't care. She wanted a flat bed, just like at home. So I stayed on the leather couch, Barb took Sherry's bed, and Sherry moved to the hospital bed, which was now hard, as Barb took her feather mattress. We put on our pajamas and settled in for the night.

Suddenly, Sherry started to laugh. I laughed. Then Barbara laughed. The three of us laughed and laughed. Finally Barbara said, "All right, what the heck are we laughing at?" That sent us into new gales of uncontrollable laughter.

Sherry finally said, "I was just imagining a nurse coming in during the night when it is dark and giving me Barbara's medication."

The next morning one of the vitamin girls arrived and gave Barb a gentle massage. Barb gave her some money to take to the temple and make merit. Barb wasn't taking the vitamins (or whatever they were) because they made her very nauseous.

After the vitamin girl left, we had the first talk about what was going on. Without saying the words or giving a time frame (Barb always insisted she didn't want a timeline on her survival), we discussed the situation. We cried together. Barb said she didn't deserve to have us here — she hadn't done enough merit in her lifetime — so we talked about all the things she had done for me over the years, such as helping set up my dress shop and walking through my alcoholism with me (I had now been sober for 38 years). Barbara had given Sher her vehicle every day when Sherry was in Thunder Bay working for one summer, and she readily offered guidance based on her experience whenever Sherry needed another opinion or felt confused.

We talked about Barb's helping villagers learn some English phrases, her hospice work, and her visits to the Thai orphanages. These were fun things, worthy things, memorable things.

She was worried about our sacrifice of coming to Thailand to be with her. We had left our families behind to fend for themselves, and this concerned her greatly. We assured her that it was no sacrifice; it was an honour. Our families had insisted that we go to Thailand to be with her. Sherry and I knew this was the truth.

Although it was an emotional conversation, it was heartwarming and so needed. We removed her sense of guilt regarding our being with her, and I think she was finally at peace with our presence.

Wanchai arrived with our dinners, but the smell of the food bothered Barb, so we opened the slider and turned the air-conditioner on high. Her tummy was very delicate, and the slightest whiff of heavy spices set it churning. We ate on the balcony with the door open so that we could still interact with her. Dinner was excellent but far too much for one meal. Leftovers went into the fridge for the next day. Wanchai left around 8:30 p.m. after sitting with Barb.

She was nauseous the whole time Wanchai visited and could not eat her broth and rice. I ordered a nausea shot, hoping that this would settle her stomach, but at midnight she vomited. This was a bad night for us, after a very emotional day.

Some days were filled with pain and sickness, and then other days found her joking and congenial. As soon as the pain began to escalate, her patch was raised to try to keep the morphine level as low as possible. Morphine side effects could be pretty ugly.

The day before, she had held her arm up and inspected the bony append-age with its loose, thin, wrinkly skin. She flicked her fingers on the sagging undercarriage a few times. Then, as she flopped her arm back and forth, she said, "What the hell is this?!"

Once again Barb's port blew, but the anesthesiologist was able to put a new one into her right arm and a splint on the elbow so she couldn't move it and irritate the port site. This port should last five days, and after that they could try a new vein if they could find one that wasn't collapsed.

Barb was nowhere near giving up or just going home, but she was getting very tired. The new patch was working well along with morphine by port injection every four hours. Her pain was more under control.

I had great difficulty keeping my emotions at bay, and I'm sure the nurses suspected that my bloodshot eyes were the result of something no good. One morning, my tears brimmed over and I turned away to hide my feelings. Barbara called me over to her and then hit me on the head with an empty water bottle. The bonk was accompanied with "Stop that!"

Sherry went to the walking market with Wanchai for a couple of hours. The usual occurred; he ate, and Sher shopped. The night markets were always such a source of fun for us. Barb and I had wandered about them regularly in times past. The market wasn't necessarily about the bargains, although we always bartered and bought; it was about the crowds, the music, the excitement, and the food. Barb and I both wanted Sherry to have this wonderful Chiang Mai experience.

We had a good night — despite Barb's cracking cough — as her sleep-ing pills were working well and the nausea medication was also on point. I needed to go to Doi Saket for clean clothes and some supplies, so I decided to go in a tuk-tuk the next day and then come back with Wanchai, while Sherry stayed with Barb.

In the morning, I showered, dressed in soiled clothes, and packed for Doi Saket. I was taking dirty clothes home to wash or store. Num, our tuk-tuk driver, picked me up at noon. I took Sher's purchases from the walking market with me — bags and bags of treasures for her boys.

When I arrived at Doi Saket, I noticed that the housekeeper had taken over the house as if it were her own. She often brought her baby, La, to work. Baby dishes were everywhere, and baby items were in my bedroom. The house was a mess, the floors were not swept, and dishes were in the sink. I think she was a bit embarrassed, as she hadn't been expecting me. She quickly began to wash the floors.

The house didn't feel right without Barbara, as was evident from the unusual behavior of the housekeeper, who was usually very diligent in her duties. I was critical because of how sharply it contrasted with how the house had been kept when Barb was there. I would have to make merit for my criticism.

Wanchai said we were leaving Doi Saket for the hospital at 3:00 p.m., so I had to hustle. Barb had given me several chores to complete, one of which was to e-mail a change-of-beneficiary request to Barb's employer. The balance of her work pension would now go to her granddaughter. It needed to be done on her computer, which was at home. Later, she signed the official form.

I packed up a suitcase of clean clothes, and Wanchai dropped me off at the hospital at 4:00 p.m. Barb had been in agony all afternoon. Nothing was working, and Sherry was very happy to see me. Sometimes the pain medication just did not do its job.

That evening, Wanchai and his sister Pum came to the hospital. Barbara had received some medical help and a long massage, so she was feeling better. She was very close to Wanchai's sister, and they had a lovely visit.

Sometimes we lived one day at a time; some days, one hour at a time. When they left, Barbara didn't want to take her sleeping pills, with a disastrous result. Often, with the sleeping pills, she slept through blood pressure checks, but when the nurses came in at 2:00 a.m. to take her blood pressure, they accidently woke us all up. Barb was in pain until morning when meds kicked in. Then she slept. She needed this rest.

Wanchai came at 5:00 p.m. with chicken soup, and we had a wonderful laughter-filled evening, as Barb had spent most of the day sleeping. That evening her IV blew again, with the infusion going straight into her arm instead of the bloodstream. The doctor decided to give her veins a rest and to leave the nourishment IV off for a while, administering meds orally or with an injection through a new port. All three of us were asleep by 10:00 p.m. We were never bored in our voluntary prison.

At 5:30 a.m., we were awakened with a nice poop accident. It meant shower time and a hair wash for Barb, which was a much easier job with no IV pole. Sher showered the two of them, and I remade the bed. We had a system.

Later in the morning, Barb had another accident, this time missing the bedding but nailing the floor beautifully from bed to bathroom. Sher took care of Barb, and I called for housekeeping, as this was not a simple clean up. In no time at all, Barb was back in bed, all tidied up. The good news was that there were no bowel blockages. Barb happily went to sleep.

The housekeeping staff came in twice a day as a regular routine just to do the floors. They wet-mopped once and dry-mopped once each day as well as doing the usual dusting and disinfecting the bathroom. These young girls giggled and chatted as they worked, and they loved to clean our room, especially after we gave them chocolates.

When Wanchai was visiting once, Barb gave me money and told Sherry and me to go to the bakery to purchase pastries for the nursing staff, which we did. The nurses were so surprised to receive the huge basket of sweet goodies, enough for three shifts. Once Wanchai brought a huge basket of cheese and fruit for the staff.

The nurses all wore crisp white uniforms with proper nursing caps, just as ours did decades ago. All the staff could be identified by their clothing, except doctors, who wore anything from scrubs to three-piece suits. A sense of pride existed on the floor and in the building. We all belonged to a sort of family.

Sherry went to visit Suan Dok Temple just down the street. Barbara insisted that Sherry visit this special temple, and before she went, Barb schooled her in proper behavior, etiquette, and attire. Sher said she was a little nervous because she didn't want to embarrass herself by doing the wrong thing. She did just fine and ended up talking to a young monk from Myanmar for an hour and a half and then spent almost an hour in the temple. On the way home, she purchased some items from the Hill Tribe Store.

While Sherry was gone, Barb and I discussed what still needed to come from the house and things that needed to be distributed. I wrote everything down. We walked down the hall and sat on the leather couch by the fountain and the window overlooking the city. In true Barbara style, she wouldn't leave the room until she had brushed her hair and put on lipstick.

We could see the temple on the mountain, Doi Suthep, which we had visited on many occasions. The sunlight reflected off the gold *chedi,* giving the distant temple a mystical appearance. Wat Phra That Doi Suthep was on the top of Doi Suthep Mountain, about 15 miles from the city center. The first *chedi* was built in 1383, and all the supplies had to be carried up to the summit at 3,542 feet above sea level. The road was finally built in 1935. Monks and workers carried everything up by hand, through the jungle, before the road was built. The long, windy road trip to the top took about half an hour by car, and I always got carsick if I didn't take motion sickness medication. The visit was still worth it.

The first time that Barbara and I visited this temple, we climbed the 309 steps from the base of the temple to the top (guarded by flashy Naga dragons), not knowing that a funicular (cable car) was available for a small charge. We were reminded later that one did not make merit by using the funicular. This was the holiest temple in Chiang Mai, towering over Chiang Mai University.

When Barbara and I returned from our walk down the hall, Barb got a bad attack of vertigo. Strong emotions often triggered these attacks, as did sleeping on her side.

When Sherry came back from her trip, she amused us by dancing around the room as she told us about her visit to the temple.

Most days we laughed more than we cried.

Barbara's bedside table was covered in an assortment of items: some were medication, some were personal, such as her glasses. Sherry had brought some dark-chocolate-covered cranberry treats from home, and when Barb saw us snacking on them, she wanted some.

"Of course," I said. "How many would you like for starters?"

"Just put four or five in that little saucer, and I will have them later."

I picked out a half a dozen of the little indulgences and placed them in a kitchen saucer, next to her salve, the carminative (to relieve gas), and her antacid tablets. A short time later, our jovial pain doctor came in for his daily visit and he spied them. He was in charge of all of her medication, and we noticed he was looking at the saucer with a puzzled expression. Finally he asked, "What are the black pills?" He was pretty sure he hadn't ordered any black pills. Barb told him what they were, and we all laughed when he popped two of them into his mouth, just to make sure. He liked them.

At 3:30 in the morning, Barb had an accident, and within forty minutes she was showered and back in a clean bed. We were getting very good at this. And quick.

She had no IV line, as her arm veins had phlebitis. Everything was getting a rest. She expressed a lot of very funny childlike behavior now, lots of face-making and baby talk. We played all the games and laughed with her and joined in. One of her favourite games was to put her Winnie the Pooh comforter over her head and then say, "Find me! Find me!"

Barbara loved the light hospital comforters provided for warmth. They were from the children's floor, as nothing like that was available for adults. She found the blankets too heavy. Whenever her comforter was soiled, I would quickly go to the nurses' station to tell them, and they immediately found another for her. They seemed to understand, and there was never an argument or a delay. We were very amused when I opened up a new comforter after Winnie needed changing and the new one was covered in dolls with "Barbie" written all over.

Barb giggled, "A Barbie for Barbie!" We took pictures. Then she suddenly became very serious. Drugs caused this behavior.

The pain doctor had told us about Pansao, the temple on the hospital grounds, and the monk, Pra Maharwon, who turned water into glass. He urged us to go to this temple to experience this event for ourselves. Barb was very weak and her weight was 43 kilos, but we were given permission to take her to the temple on hospital property.

We were without IV pole, so it seemed like the perfect opportunity, and although the day was very warm, it still looked like a comfortable wheelchair push. So Barbara "decorated" (put on make-up), and we borrowed a wheelchair from the hospital, knowing that we had to be there before 1:00

p.m. The doctor called to make sure this monk would be available at that time. He came to this temple several times a year.

We rolled Barb's wheelchair to the back of the hospital, and using the doctor's written directions, wound our way past hairdressers, several restaurants, and various businesses.

Sher pushed Barb in the wheelchair while I held a big umbrella over her head to protect her from the sun, and away we went, bumpiddy-bump down the back streets, until we reached the temple. It was wonderful to get out into the fresh air and walk beneath the tropical trees, basking in the warmth of the Thai sun.

We arrived at the temple at the same time as about a dozen Thais and pulled the wheelchair up the stairs, but Barbara walked up the steps and into the main chamber. We knew it would be all right for Barb to sit in the wheelchair once in the temple. Everyone else sat on the floor. They were expecting us.

Parts of the grounds were under renovation, but this building's renovation was complete. Pra Maharwon arrived. He was a very small, slim man, very ordinary looking, even though his sleeveless burgundy robes suggested a higher calling.

When a monk blessed people in a temple, it was common practice for the monk to tie a white or coloured string around the recipient's wrist. These San Sin bracelets were thought to bring good luck, and they had to be left on until they naturally fell off; cutting them would cut off the good luck. Sometimes monks would make special braided wristbands.

First Pra Maharwon blessed the whole group. Nothing unusual happened. Then he began to bless individuals, and when he dipped his blessing whisk in the holy water, he gave it a shake and flicked it over each person in front of him. Beautiful tiny pieces of colored glass came out. Some people had spread clean cloths on the floor to catch the glass. Barb, Sher, and I were each blessed individually and given our wrist string, and after each blessing, we collected the glass all around us, about forty pieces.

After making merit by donation, we girls were given some little bags in which to store the glass pieces we had collected. Barb got the biggest piece — green, her birthstone. Pink was of some special significance, but there were only two tiny pieces of pink.

We had no idea how he did this. I looked in the water vessel when I was being blessed, and it looked like water to me. The blessing was all very beautiful. A strange experience, this was, one perhaps to just accept and enjoy.

Once outside, we called our Tuk-tuk driver to come and get us, and Num went to the wrong temple, so we had a long wait in the heat. The upside was that we were out of the hospital. Finally the tuk-tuk arrived and Num loaded up the collapsible wheelchair. We thought we were going back to the hospital, but Barbara ordered us to take to her to the Hill Tribe Store so she could shop! It was about a half kilometer from the hospital. There, she bought a doll for her great-granddaughter and a hat that made her look like Mom.

Back at the hospital we washed her, fed her some pasta (two spoons full), hydrated her, and put her to bed. It was a truly glorious day. We were so grateful that her two doctors encouraged her to do this if she felt well enough. Even though it was very hot, it was such a wonderful outing, and Barb enjoyed herself immensely, as did Sherry and I. We were making memories. Barb booked the tuk-tuk for the next day.

Although Barb was still tired after a good night's sleep, probably from the day before, she was determined to go to Wat Chedi Luang for the flower festival. This very famous temple was in the middle of the moat square, not too far from the hospital. There was a special market going on at the temple, so our driver drove us there and stayed in the shade in his tuk-tuk while we rolled the wheelchair around the grounds. Sherry sent a water offering up to the *chedi* top, and Barb bought towels for the restaurant. We stopped and had an ice cream cone and just enjoyed the ambience.

At 1:00 p.m., we left the temple to find a "red shirt" store, as Sher wanted t-shirts for the boys. But this was not to be, so we picked up dinner at the vegetarian restaurant near the temple Suan Dok by the hospital. Barb decided that she wanted flowers for her room and that she wanted to shop some more. I was very concerned about her overtiring and wanted her to go back to the hospital. She was in pain. She became very angry with me and remained so after we were settled back at the hospital.

"No one is going to tell me what to do!" she proclaimed. She was a pistol!

Sherry went to the florist and bought a lovely bouquet of orchids, eucalyptus, and chrysanthemums, but that didn't seem to help. I left the room and sat outside by the fountain for a while to give Barb a chance to cool down, which she did. We didn't speak of it again, but I made a decision to step back, even if her choice wasn't in her best interests, unless it was obviously dangerous. I wouldn't allow her to jump off the balcony, but overtiring herself would have to be her decision. This was her disease. I remembered the saying "Mind your own business." I needed to mind mine.

Right after I returned to the room, Barb had a blowout, making it to the bathroom just in time. After our usual cleaning and settling her into her bed, she cried and cried. That was very unusual behavior for her. This was all becoming too real. Her legs were aching from all the activity, so we massaged them for a long time. That night Barb slept for twelve hours.

There was no talk of going home from her doctors, and she had not asked to go home yet, although Wanchai so desperately wanted to have her at home. I think that he felt in his heart that if he could just get her home, all of this hospital/morphine/cancer/ business would go away, and they would once again be drinking coffee in the morning on the *sala,* planning the rest of their day. His heart tugged, but his head knew differently.

At noon the next day, with little warning, she lost her bowels, struggled up from the bed, which she missed. Barb hollered and Sherry caught her. They scurried toward the bathroom, with Sherry holding her up, trying to dodge the liquid pouring down Barb's legs and onto the floor like tiny muddy rivulets, while Barb tried to hold up her pajama bottoms.

It was quite a picture. I started to laugh. Sherry started to laugh. When Barb and Sherry finally hit the bathroom, Barbara, too, was laughing. Sher just stripped her and put her into the shower, then stripped and joined her. (Can you tell we'd done this before?) This time I called for housekeeping, as there was just too much for me to clean up. At least there was no bed to strip. One of our housekeepers came in with a bucket and a mop. We were still laughing our heads off, happy that Barb had missed the bed and missed Sher. Our other housekeeper opened up the door to see what was happening, took one look at the floor, and slammed the door shut, never to be seen again that day.

At least this was daytime. One night I had to strip the bed four times. I didn't know how we were going to manage at home if we got to go home. We would have to figure that out.

Sherry and I decided that it would be a good idea if Barb wore adult diapers at night in case she suddenly had an accident. She was losing some control. Sherry went across the street to the drug store and purchased what looked appropriate.

Now, we still had to convince Barb that the diapers were a good thing. We started off by naming them Big Girl Pants. She had always loved that expression, as when she was working and someone started to whine about a chore, the girls would say, "Oh, just put on your Big Girl Pants and do it!"

When Barb spotted the purchase, the look on her face told it all. She wasn't putting those things on.

We had a student doctor from the United States visiting us, so we started our performance. I put a pair on my head as a hat, and Sherry slipped a pair on over her slacks and then proceeded to dance all over the room, shaking her Big Girl Pants as only a big girl could do. We were all laughing so hard. Then Barb wore the hat, and the student put some on her arms like sleeves. It took away the stigma, and this so-useful aid just became part of our needed apparatus. The Big Girl Pants were in!

Things began to get crazier. Barb was living more and more in a strange place in her head. She wanted to go to the beach and was angry that we wouldn't take her. She wanted Wanchai to build ramps from the bedroom to the *sala.* She decided she wanted to buy a wheelchair to get around, and we couldn't tell her that she didn't have months left, only weeks. It gave her hope to believe that she had until the fall or next year.

It was so hard to watch her slipping out of reality, wanting to shop for things she would never use. She wanted us to go to Warorot Market to buy her six pairs of black pants. None of her pants fit, but she said she would be going out for dinner and to the mall and that she and Wanchai would be doing some travelling. In actuality, she was very weak and could hardly make it to the bathroom.

She was drinking lots of water but not eating. We just could not get her to eat. The pain was under control and the bad stomach was under control, but the cancer had spread to her bones, and she was complaining about bone pain. Had it already migrated to her brain? I'd been warned that would happen. I knew it would.

Barb was becoming more and more confused, and this would get worse as time progressed. But she was still very funny, and we all laughed a lot every day. We tried hard to make each day count.

I thought that we might be taking her home soon — but for how long? When we had to bring her back into the hospital, it could be to put in a central line. Her arm veins looked like they couldn't take any more needles. Her central line would have to go into the neck and straight to the heart. That would nourish the heart, but she would lose mobility.

The wheelchair-purchase idea was not a pipe dream. Barb sent Sherry to go wheelchair shopping at the three outlets across the street (and down a bit) and also to look into rental, in case Barb could go home for a few days, as was suggested by the oncologist. It cost 1,500 baht to rent for a month and up to 25,000 baht to purchase. Rental was not an option, as the chairs were wrecks. People don't typically rent in Thailand, and here's the kicker: Second-hand wheelchairs are never sold; they're given away.

A couple of hours passed, and then, after a conversation with Sherry by phone, Barb decided to get dressed and go shopping for a wheelchair. So off we went, Barb primped and propped up as I pushed her in her borrowed hospital chair, to meet with Sherry at the first drug store that sold wheelchairs. We checked out all three outlets, and Barb tried every chair in each place. I was tired just watching her. She said she would need the chair for a few months. I hid behind a display, cringing. The salespersons all spoke English, so Barb was able to barter with them and finally settled on a gorgeous chair for 17,000 baht. They ordered it to come with the bells and whistles she wanted, from another store, the next day, as she wished. It was the Lexus of wheel chairs. Now she was happy.

When we went to (Temple) Wat Pan Sao, we passed by a beautician's shop. Barb had previously asked me to cut her hair, but we had no scissors and couldn't buy haircutting scissors in the area. I was hesitant to do so, anyway. So it was off to the hairdresser's, only a block away by hospital wheelchair, so she could get a haircut. Her shoulder-length red hair was becoming difficult to handle, even with its natural curl.

We didn't have to make an appointment, as the shop advertised "drop in," and they were able to give her an operator immediately. While we waited for Barb's locks to be shortened, Sherry leaned on a glass table loaded with books. She fell to the floor when the glass top, which was covered with a plastic cover, snapped.

Well! Barb called Wanchai and explained what happened, and he talked to the owner of the shop. By the time the owner had finished, Wanchai had arranged for a new glass piece for 1,000 baht — a real scam, as the glass top was chipped and may have even been cracked. The table was very old and worth in total perhaps 300 baht. However, the shop owner smelled money and was adamant that we needed to replace the glass. Later we thought perhaps Sher should have feigned injury and that we might sue; however, that would only work in America.

After Barb's haircut, which was lovely, we rolled around to the other side of the hospital to pick up her new wheelchair and were finished by about 3:30 p.m. She was very happy with her new transportation, and she was especially pleased that she wouldn't have to use the cumbersome hospital chairs anymore.

We had a quiet dinner as Barbara slept and had a quiet evening. The oncologist told us that we could take Barb home the next day, but we had to have her back on Sunday. He said she needed a rest from the hospital. She wasn't on the IV drip and seemed to be doing fine, judging from her outings. That would give her six days at home. I went to the hospital pharmacy to fill her prescriptions in preparation for this time away from the hospital, where the ring of a buzzer brought quick medication when needed.

Barb thought she would be having chemo when she returned. The doctor wanted her to have an opportunity to put things in order and say goodbye. He called it a break from the hospital. She called it a rest period before chemo. I called it clearing her bucket list.

Sherry and I just continued to love her and help in any way we could.

Chapter Eight

"Thousands of candles can be lit from one single candle, and the life of the candle will not be shortened. Happiness never decreases by being shared."
—Gautama Buddha

WANCHAI came to pick us up at 1:00 on Monday afternoon. We were all packed, ready to go, but it took the three of us and four Thai hospital workers to get our belongings and Barbara to the truck, which was parked out front. My, we had collected a lot, and everything had to come home with us.

Once at the house, Barb happily headed for her bed, and Sher and I unpacked. When I opened the fridge, I was almost blown over. It desperately needed a cleaning and a "throw that out, it's gone bad." Keeping the fridge clean was not the housekeeper's job, and the fridge hadn't been touched for almost three weeks. Wanchai ate out and spent his evenings at the restaurant and with us in the hospital. I cleaned out the freezer as well, so everything would be fine for a while.

Wanchai saw me throwing out old food and quickly gave me strict orders not to throw out his bugs. Sure enough, there was a snack bag of bugs for him to nibble on when the mood struck. (Remember, Thais eat everything except planes and trains — not far from the truth. Once while dining out, Barbara yawned, and Wanchai popped a bug from his dish into her mouth. She didn't know what it was, chewed, and swallowed, and said it was like popcorn. However, she warned him not to do that again. He thought it was hilarious.)

Barb really pushed hard after her nap. She wanted to show everyone that she was "better." She walked in the garden, chatted with Steve, and stayed in the kitchen while I made a spaghetti dinner for Sherry and me. She ate nothing.

It was a special time for Barbara and Steve, as he wasn't able to visit the hospital easily, but he needed to come to terms with the new future, one without Barbara. They had been very good friends for a long time. They often went tuk-tuk grocery shopping together, and Barb had known Steve for as long as she had known Wanchai. She still had to use his bilingual services when she couldn't explain something to Wanchai properly. Steve was a wonderful friend to her.

Wanchai went to work that evening, and we three girls snuggled on Barb's bed and watched television until he returned so that she wouldn't be alone. That became our night time habit: Barbara was never to be alone.

So far, the hospital stay had been unbelievably inexpensive compared to a similar stay in America. Everything was included — hospital, doctors, specialists, nurses, and medications. Barb hoped that her savings would cover her illness so as not to financially burden Wanchai too much. She'd tried to enroll in the Thai medical system when she moved to Chiang Mai but wasn't accepted because of her long-existing thyroid condition and high blood pressure. She took medications for both, and they were under control.

While we were living at the hospital, Wanchai and Steve designed and built a huge waterfall where the old one was but three times taller. It was shaped with wire and concrete and had water cascading down the center. Plants were placed in various pockets. It was impressive. Hired workers did most of the heavy labour, although Wanchai worked physically alongside the laborers.

On our first full day home, four fan banana trees were to arrive with some smaller trees as well to make a vegetation wall on the side of the driveway beside our bedroom. It would give privacy from the land next door, which Wanchai thought he might develop one day. Working on the beautiful gardens was how he managed to cope.

My understanding was that once Barb was re-admitted to hospital next Sunday, she wouldn't be coming home. She rarely passed water now and didn't drink water unless we chased her with a glass and straw. She would soon be dehydrated again. On that first day home, she ate two spoons of yogurt and one-eighth of a cup of spaghetti with one bite of cheese. She said that she felt like having salty, or cold, or hot, or sour, or any other concoction, and I tried to get whatever she wanted to her quickly, as I knew the mood would be gone soon, and then she would feel like eating nothing. She was taking in so few calories. Sherry froze Ensure nutrition drinks into little cubes, but a serving was made from eight scoops, and Barb would consume the equivalent of one scoop or less in a day. She was slowly starving.

This was common with pancreatic cancer. So far, bowels were moving but with diarrhea; however, we had a pattern now, so no more night time blowouts. I often had to change her bed in the hospital several times in a night while Sherry washed her in the shower. We totally took care of her personal needs. It was a dignity thing. In the hospital, the nursing staff was supportive and at our beck and call. I made up tracking sheets monitoring food and medications and taped them to the cupboard so we could see easily what was happening. I did the same at home.

Barbara experienced paranoia now and confusion, all part of the morphine regime. She verbally went after me one day, and the next day she went after Sherry. It was over nothing, so we figured out how to stay out of the line of fire. Barb quickly forgot what she had said or what she was upset about. She wanted to go to a Chinese doctor whom she thought would arrange for her to have chemo and kill the cancer.

Wanchai also came up with cancer cures, like drinking glasses of lime juice. He prepared a glass of the juice; she had a few sips and then threw up all the food and water that she had consumed during the day, plus more. She tried hard to please him as he struggled to save her.

Barb was so grateful that we were there, and Sherry and I both understood that the time would come when that might disappear. We got it.

Sherry and I cleaned up the bedrooms and prepared a laundry basket for the laundress while Barb was very busy, bustling about the house and the yard. She had lots of energy and even ate some scrambled eggs and a part of a piece of toast. She did too much, but there was no holding her down. She must have known that this was going to be her last stint in her home.

The yard was beautiful and lush, and in the afternoon, the four fan banana trees arrived. They were about 30 feet tall, and a special truck with a hoist was used. Workers dug the holes first and then the hoist lowered each tree into place. They were planted along the side of the driveway outside our bedroom, and they were so gorgeous.

I cleaned out Barb's clothes closets and cupboards. It was a big job, mostly emotional. I colour-blocked all of her tops and separated what she wanted to go home to Canada with us from what needed to go to specific people. She was very tiny, as were her clothes, but she knew that some things would serve no purpose staying in Thailand. She had so many garments, the equivalent of about 12 feet of holding bar just for the tops, including jackets. All of her folded bottoms were in a very large shelved dresser. I arranged them in piles by colour as well. Many bottoms were just too large for her now, so I removed them. Barb sat on the bed and directed traffic.

Afterward, she wanted to get out, so we packed up her wheelchair with some supplies and rolled down the road, first to Wanchai's sister's to show Sherry her beautiful home. Barb's previous housekeeper was there, and she joyfully gave us a tour. This home was outstanding and huge. Wanchai's sister, Pum, had pretty much completed renovations, and the teak floors, stairs, and rails were unbelievable in their beauty. Sherry took pictures.

Then we went a bit further down the road, to Art's home, but his mom, Noi, was at work, so we had some refreshing cold water with his grand-mother. It was close to 100°F outside. She was so happy to see us. We spoke no Thai, and she spoke no English, yet we had a lovely visit.

Three generations lived in the home that Wanchai had built many years ago for his family. Typically there was no pressured hot water in Thai homes, so water was warm or cool for showering. Barb and Wanchai's home had a full hot water system, so when Art spent weekends with them, he had hot showers. He would grin and say, "Like in Canada!"

We continued down the road seeking township garbage bags from a grocery store, but neither of the nearby stores had any left. That was how one paid for the twice-a-week garbage collection. Garbage went into these purchased and labeled black garbage bags, and they were put out onto the street for collection by a big truck.

Barbara thought there was a road to a small lake nearby, so we continued on our journey, looking for the way to this lake, when suddenly shouting came from a huge yard on our left.

"Bahbella! Bahbella!" Barbara was well-known in the neighbourhood. Wanchai and his family had lived in the area for generations. Village women were gathered in the yard, preparing food for the Festival of the Spirits, which was tomorrow. Wanchai was elsewhere, helping with the organizing. Sherry pushed Barbara's wheelchair into the yard, and a half a dozen women sporting huge smiles greeted us.

We were quickly ushered into lawn chairs and brought cold water. Some women were kneading dough, others were removing the meat from coconuts (one man was at this chore as well), and others were cutting banana leaves into parallelograms. Each piece of leaf was folded around rice, spices, and chicken or pork, and then the wrap was roasted. One would eat the inside, not the leaf. Wanchai often brought these delicious wraps for our dinner. Once again, the only language needed was that of caring and camaraderie. Smiles were abundant, and Barbara's very small Thai vocabulary was all that was necessary. We *waid.*

The *wai* is a Thai greeting with palms together and fingers pointing up, accompanied by a small head bow. There are etiquette stipulations as well, determining who should *wai* first, the height of the *wai,* and the depth of the bow. We tried our best not to be rude.

"Sabai dii mai?" (How are you?) Barbara asked everyone. Sherry and I knew how to greet, putting hands together in a *wai* and saying, "Sawatdee-ka," which was the *aloha* of Thailand. We also knew to say "Khob khun Kaa," or "thank you," when we left. Politeness in Thailand goes a long way. Thais even treat strangers with respect, but we were considered family and so were given exceptional attention. We were made to feel very special, because we were Wanchai's Barbara and Barbara's Canada family.

Suddenly Wanchai was driving by on his motorbike, and when he realized we were there, he came back and joined us, so happy that Barb was out and having fun.

He chatted with some of the villagers. (I'm sure they asked about Barbara's health, as her name kept popping up.) When it was time for Wanchai to leave in order to finish his chore of placing directional flags to show where the celebration would occur tomorrow, Barb got up out her wheelchair and climbed onto the back of the motorbike. She took the flags in her hand and waved them in the air. Both Wanchai and Barbara were grinning, and the two of them took off on the bike. The villagers were astounded. So were Sherry and I.

We started to leave, pushing the now-empty wheelchair, when I heard, "Chok dee, pee saao," which means, "Good luck, older sister." They knew how this was going to go. Family in Thailand took care of family. Barbara had taught many of them some English phrases, and she always supported the local businesses. They genuinely cared about her.

Sherry and I pushed the empty wheelchair home in the heat, laughing at this turn of events. When we arrived at the house about fifteen minutes later, Barb said, "So, what took you so long?" It was a wonderful afternoon.

At 6:00 the next morning, Barb was outside wandering about her yard and gardens. This frightened Wanchai, as his grandmother had wandered her property two days before she died.

Barbara asked me for her blood pressure pills, which she had not needed for six months. She accepted that she did not need them anymore when I explained this to her.

Our tuk-tuk arrived at 10:00 a.m., and Num took us to Kad Suan Kaew Mall. Barbara wanted to go to the large grocery store there, and she went on a shopping spree.

I pushed her in the wheelchair, and Sherry pushed the shopping cart while Barb loaded it up. She bought many things she would not use, but oh, how she loved to shop! Therefore, small water bottles ("I need little bottles for when I travel"), two dozen jars of baby food ("I think I might like this baby fruit"), many containers of different kinds of juice ("This juice will be good for me"), cereal boxes ("I wonder what this tastes like"), coffee (for Wanchai), ice cube trays, two large packages of straws, pudding, and anything else that was within arm's reach ended up in the cart as I pushed her down the aisle. As she reached for something new, I tried to put back some of the things in the cart. It was like shopping with a toddler.

We bought a cake mix, some canned pineapple, and brown sugar because she wanted me to make a pineapple upside-down cake. That special cake was a favourite that our mom used to make. Then Barb decided she wanted strawberries and whipped cream (there were no strawberries, as they aren't a Thai fruit), but by the time we got into the fruit area, she had forgotten about it — she had spotted an ice cream cone sign just out the door at KFC.

We went through the till, paid for the groceries, stopped at the bank machine at the door for some more cash, and headed for the KFC. Sherry and I ordered a soft-serve ice cream cone and one for our driver, Num. Barb ordered a cone and a chocolate ice drink for herself.

We rushed out of the mall looking for our driver, who was not in his usual parking spot, so I searched around the corner while Barb phoned him to say, "We are ready. Come now." His ice cream was melting.

When he arrived, I handed Num his cone, just about the time that Barb had a blowout. She was wearing what we affectionately still called "Big Girl Pants," but she was worried about leaking onto her new wheelchair. Sherry ran and bought some more adult diapers, as we had neglected to bring a change with us, and we wheeled Barb across the huge mall to the washroom area. An attendant ushered us into a handicapped-accessible room, and we were easily able to change her with no harm to her chair.

She said, "Oh, my God! I'm a baby again!" We laughed and laughed.

Home we went, loaded with groceries, but now Barb was very tired and in pain. We always had morphine with us for a boost dose, but sometimes it wasn't enough and bed rest was necessary.

On the way home, Barbara shared that Wanchai had told her he was going to see their Buddhist monk Mitt, from their temple, to arrange for "the box" and the covering housing. He had cried as he told her. It would take time for the solid teak box to be made.

We arrived at home around 4:00 p.m. Barb rested for a while as Sherry and I put the groceries away. Then Wanchai drove us to the Festival of the Spirits, which was a village celebration in the very place we had visited the day before. Huge tents had been erected to protect the celebrators from the sun. There were tables and chairs about and a live band, and villagers were dressed in beautiful brightly coloured costumes. There were foods and drinks and once again I was reminded that Thais love to party.

The music was like Thai rock and roll — very upbeat — and everyone was dancing. We were again ushered in and handed cold drinks (alcohol would appear later for some revelers). This celebrating began at 10:00 in the morning and carried on nonstop. The dancers switched and so did the musicians, but the party never stopped. After about ten minutes, one of the lady organizers, who just loved Barb, grabbed Sherry and encouraged her to get up and dance with the Thai dancers. Barb went to an elder, made merit, and was blessed while Sher danced, and then they got after me. And so I danced. And danced. And danced. Sherry never stopped.

Suddenly Barb raised herself out of her wheelchair and grabbed Wanchai, and she danced and danced. Sherry recorded it on her iPhone. This woman, who couldn't have walked to this celebration, danced with her villagers and neighbors. I was reminded of an Erin Hanson quotation that my dear friend Elizabeth had sent me, which said, "What if I fall?" It continued, "Oh, but darling, what if you fly?" Barbara flew that night.

The villagers were astounded. They all knew how ill she was. Spending some time with her villagers was so important to Barb. This gave huge face, or respect, for Wanchai — the fact that Barbara and her "Canada" family were there to dance and celebrate with them.

Just as suddenly, Barb was tired. We poured her into her wheelchair, and Sher and I rolled her home, leaving Wanchai to stay a bit longer and help clean up. I made the pineapple upside-down cake she wanted, and she had two big pieces. Wanchai went to work, and we three girls were all asleep by 8:00 p.m.

We were off and running again in the tuk-tuk, wheelchair strapped to the back, at 10:30 in the morning. Originally we were going to stop at the gold stores on highway 118, which were not that far from home. Barb wanted the three of us to buy gold chains for Sherry's boys, as this year would have their golden birthdays (turning 9 on the 9th and 11 on the 11th). Instead of our usual quick route to Chiang Mai, we wanted to go on the back roads, or *sois,* so that we could see more of the countryside. It would take longer, but it avoided the fast traffic, and wandering beside rice fields, homes, and small businesses would be more relaxing.

On our left as we turned around a corner was a Thai crematorium. "Stop! Stop!" Barbara hollered.

Our driver, Num, finally did so, reluctantly. "Why you stop here?" he asked. "Nothing here. We go."

Many Thais are quite superstitious and don't even look at a crematorium, as was evident from the upset of our driver. Yet Thais, being mostly Buddhist, are typically cremated with great ceremony. It was the spirits that hang around that bothered them.

"Just stay here and wait for us!" Barbara commanded. Sherry and I were fascinated and followed Barb onto the grounds. There, Barbara explained what each area was for, what typically would happen. This was not their village crematorium, so it was not personal, but of course, it was. Barbara was setting the scene for Sherry and me and walking through what would be her own experience at a later time. It was surreal and yet comforting, like sharing a secret.

We climbed back into the tuk-tuk, our driver continuing to face only forward, and with a puff of exhaust smoke we were once again chugging down the road.

We needed to go all the way into the city, as Wanchai had requested a special chain and lock and we had said we would pick it up for him. The hardware store was close to his restaurant, as was the laundress, so we decided to pick up our laundry as well. When we arrived at the laundry, Barb had a blowout, and luckily we were parked at Wanchai's restaurant. Num tracked down the cook to open up the restaurant so we could use the washroom. We came prepared, so we were in good shape in no time. Barb said goodbye to her laundress, who had done her laundry for eight years, and to the cook, whom she had known for almost as long. Then we went to the fruit market, and she said goodbye to all the merchants who had witnessed Wanchai and Barbara's love story for many years. That was when I realized Barb was saying her goodbyes without saying goodbye.

Finally we arrived at Warorot Market on the Ping River, the oldest market in Chiang Mai. We managed to scrounge up enough baht to purchase the chains for the boys. Barb was exhausted, but we still had to stop at the temple to deliver the big bank full of coins that she had been collecting for years. She needed to do it herself; that was huge merit. Mitt, her monk, was happy to see us and blessed us all.

I had been with her, months before, when she told Mitt that she had cancer. "Where?" he had asked.

"Here, on my pancreas."

"They will fix?"

"No, Mitt, it is too late."

I saw his eyes fill. "I will bless you now." He said his temple words that day, and tied the strings on our wrists. Mitt was a very important part of Barb and Wanchai's life, and a good friend. He and Wanchai were both educated in this very temple when youngsters, and Mitt stayed on as a practicing monk, while Wanchai chose the life of a Buddhist citizen. Wanchai told me once that he had begun to notice girls and so he had to leave.

Every day Barb pushed herself at an unbelievable rate. "Today I called our driver, and we are going . . ." always just for an hour, but it would turn into four or five. Yet when we arrived home, she did not go to bed. We would wander about the yard. We went into the pool every afternoon for an hour or so, and she loved that.

Once home, after our last day on the run, we decided to go into the swimming pool to relax, as it was very hot outside. The water was lovely. Sherry and I enjoyed it immensely, but Barb was zoned out, hanging onto the side of the pool, unable to interact with Sherry, Steve, and me. We often lost her now for longer periods of time. It had been an exhausting day for all of us. I didn't know how she was still moving.

After we put Barb to bed, tired out and morphined up, Sherry and I washed the two dogs. We leashed them to a shade tree, and they were both very well-behaved as we scrubbed them with tick soap. We picked dozens of ticks off them — *soi* dogs seem to not be bothered with the ticks (a *soi* is a narrow, winding back road that wanders through villages or neighbourhoods, and Thai dogs, who are often called *soi dogs,* wander these roads). Wanchai came home at 10:00 after closing the restaurant early. It was slow season.

During that six-day hiatus from the hospital, Barb did everything from giving gardening orders and supervising as Sherry and I prepared a snack to dragging us off in a tuk-tuk with her wheelchair tied to the back so that we could get groceries, visit people, attend a festival, go to temple, make merit, pick up laundry, buy some gifts, and end each day in the pool.

We had a wonderful activity-filled few days and a welcomed respite from the hospital. Every time I begged Barb to slow down, she gave me the evil eye and told me what was next on the agenda.

Chapter Nine

"Three things cannot be hidden forever:
the sun, the moon, and the truth."
—Gautama Buddha

THE next morning at 5:00 a.m., Barbara hit the wall. She was due back at the hospital and she needed to be there, as she was now very ill. She'd had a bad night and was up a lot, and finally she climbed into bed with Sherry and me. Barb said that she felt different, sick but no pain. We three huddled together in bed, knowing that this was a new path. Barbara hadn't vomited the whole time we were at home. She had been running on adrenaline, or Finnish *sisu* (we were, after all, Finnish). *Sisu* has no direct translation, but it's like a kind of determination, a bravery or resilience. A Finn might say, "It doesn't take *sisu* to go to the North Pole; it takes *sisu* to stand at the door when the bear is on the other side."

This was a huge shift, as Barb now had no energy, no ambition, no interest. Wanchai drove us to the hospital, and this time I packed clothing into my large blue suitcase, on spinning wheels, which would be easier to handle than many small bags. We were in Room #1423, at the other end of the hall and right across from the router, so we didn't have to go into the hall to e-mail or surf the net. We needed accessible Wi-Fi, and now had it.

Barb vomited twice that day, once at noon and once in the evening, and had not passed water for two days. She was being given lots of nausea medications, which weren't working well. Her pain doctor changed all her medication to IV, except milk of magnesia for constipation, which had set in with a vengeance. We rearranged the room so that Barb's bed was in the middle, allowing easy night time access for either Sherry or me. We could get to Barb fast.

Sherry picked up curried chicken from the bakery in the morning after we arrived, so dinner was delicious. Food became a focal point of our day, but at times I felt guilty enjoying a Thai dish, knowing that Barbara could not. The guilt came from me, never from anything she said. I think she liked to watch us delighting in a new taste, and she encouraged us to try different foods. It seemed as if we were inheriting her life in Thailand in some small way.

Wanchai talked in great detail that evening about his gardens, his trees, and his plans for the property. Barbara listened and enjoyed the conversation, contributing to the dialogue when Wanchai's English vocabulary failed him. He spoke of the delicate white flowering Leelawadee trees, which he had planted for Barbara; "a woman beautifully adorned," the English translation of the name, was his fading sweetheart. He needed a distraction, and for him, that was usually his gardens; it used to be Barbara. The evening was very loving for all of us.

After Wanchai left, it was a late bedtime for all of us, and Sherry was still up at 2:00 a.m. I finally said to her, "Honey, you need to go to sleep. Staff will be in here at 6:00 a.m."

Barbara responded with "Rene, you need to get your own hotel room." She sure could make me chuckle.

Barb was very noisy in her sleep that night, with fluids gathering in her throat area. We propped her up so she would be more comfortable. She always needed pillows surrounding her now.

After six days at home, things were progressing as expected now that we were back at Sriphat Hospital. It had been a wonderful hiatus, and Barb had been able to accomplish most of the things that she was bent on doing. Was this part of her closure? Does a dying person feel like she needs closure? Is closure simply acceptance? When does it change from fighting for your life to fighting for your death?

I had not thought much about closure, or what it was, or if I would ever find it. After Mom died, I remember having difficulty going into her bank, which was not my bank. I did not like entering our favourite coffee shop. I stopped volunteering at the art gallery because it was painful to be there without her. None of this ever changed. I would be driving home and suddenly remember something we did or something she said, and the sobs would be there instantly. At times I pulled off the road. Was this all because I hadn't had closure? Closure meant "conclusion." How could this ever be concluded, like Mom was over, like she didn't exist? I had a lot of work to do on understanding death, and now there was Barbara.

Sherry would be here until near the end of June, while I hoped to stay until it was finished. How could someone's life be finished? How could I stay? How could I not stay?

Barb was getting weaker, couldn't eat, and vomited a lot but was in little pain due to very strong medications. Sherry and I took care of her by choice. The nurses and staff were wonderful. It was so different here, as family just lived in the hospital, coming and going as was convenient and needed. We were in the second most expensive hospital. The most expensive one was what most foreigners used, as the staff all spoke English. Our doctors spoke English, and there were always nurses around who could speak English, so we have never had a problem.

I was careful to stay away from details of the prognosis when Barb and I talked about her illness. She still didn't want to know. When the oncologist came in to visit, she questioned him. "When can I have chemotherapy again?" she asked.

"I think you have a fifty-fifty chance of being strong enough for chemo," was the reply. "We can do some testing, and if it is all right, we can try, or we can wait until tomorrow. It is your choice. I don't think you are strong enough."

"If I get stronger, can I have chemo?"

The doctor responded, "Of course, but it is not likely you will get stronger."

"I suspected that." Barb no longer sounded hopeful. She looked away.

"I think it is best to allow the natural progression to take place and concentrate on staying comfortable."

I wrote down his words in my journal. His statement was a huge shock to Barb, who at times lived in a fantasy world that did not include cancer. For some reason, she was fixated on chemo either saving her or giving her an additional six months. I knew it couldn't, as did the oncologist, but he always did his best to placate her. This was a strange dance that the two of them did, Barbara questioning and waiting for chemotherapy, which was going to save her, and her oncologist humoring her with empty promises of "tomorrow,

tomorrow." I couldn't ask the oncologist questions in front of Barbara. Rules for secrets were always in play. She demanded protection.

After the oncologist left, Sherry went to the temple, made merit for Barb, and bought a coffee mug for me, as I'd forgotten to bring one from home. Now I could have a cup of decaf. I had bought a jar of decaf from the market when we all went shopping, as restaurants in Thailand typically did not serve it.

Wanchai was so emotional that night. He hadn't slept much the night before and had spent the day looking at photographs of Barb and him building the house, of them holidaying together, of Mom in Thailand, and of Bob and me visiting. He talked about Phi Phi Island and the fun we'd had before all this tragedy took front and center. The only one not crying was Barb, who had just had 5 milliliters of morphine and was staring at the wall.

Wanchai said, "We have house, truck, bike, furniture, everything. Now is all gone. All for nothing." When he left, he was crying hard. I walked him to the elevator and tried to console him, but what could I say that would change anything?

Barb made things up (part of the disease) and changed what the doctor ordered. For example, when the doctor said, "No drugs by mouth, all by IV," she insisted on asking for some medication orally and then couldn't keep it down. She tried so hard to take as few drugs as possible. The pain doctor said, "Morphine every four hours," and she still would wait five or six hours until she was in terrible pain. It wasn't our place to insist. It still was her disease and her body. But I hated it when she was in pain, and who knew how I would handle this?

Her oxygen level was lower than normal but wasn't dangerous yet. Her voice was getting hoarse from all the vomiting. Wanchai said her eyes were hollow and she was no longer there, and I had noticed that too. Then suddenly she would be back and clearheaded and funny. I was truly living one day at a time, maybe for the first time in my life. How blessed was I to be able to help her on this journey, and how blessed was I to have my supportive family!

That almost sleepless night was bad for me. The nurses were in at 6:00 for the start of morning procedures. The oncologist came in at 12:15, his usual cheery self, which Barbara mimicked after he left. She was very good at that.

"We will see tomorrow," was his response once again, regarding her regular request for chemo.

Barb was very comfortable acting out toward me, as she knew I wouldn't throw her under the bus. She trusted me. I was concerned about double-dosing the milk of magnesia, which could give her bad cramps, and argued with her, but Sherry said, "Give it to her, Mom. If she gets the cramps, so what? We'll just deal with it then."

Barb was sure that the lack of diarrhea was what was causing the daily vomiting. It was, in fact, the cancer growths in her abdomen that caused it, as the doctor told her, but she refused to believe it. Barb still thought that she was going to die but not for six months.

Every day we lost a little more of her, and then suddenly she would shine through and would enjoy hearing Sherry and me telling stories. Barb would laugh and smile. She tried so hard to stay connected. Sher and I sat on the side of her bed for a long time in conversation, and Barb smiled. I talked about our childhood, the wonderful memories. There was so much good in our lives.

She finally fell asleep at 5:30 p.m. after we washed her. We gave Barb "bird baths" now, as she was too weak to shower. Sherry thought she might rally one more time.

That evening after he visited with Barb, Wanchai and I had a long talk. He didn't want her to suffer. He would rather that she be at the hospital with help from doctors than at home, where he was afraid that she would suffer pain without enough help. He understood that she had only weeks left.

I wanted to know if he wanted her to come home to die when the time came. He said to do whatever she wanted. He would take care of all the "funeral" arrangements, and I would do whatever he asked. He wanted Sherry to stay longer, but I managed to get through to him that she had two little boys who needed her. He wanted to know if Bob was okay. I said that we wrote every day and we missed each other but we were managing. These were hard conversations for both of us.

We were all asleep by 10:00 p.m., with a short interruption for morphine at 11:00, and we three slept eight hours.

At 10:00 a.m. Barb woke up when she heard me talking about the cool water in the shower instead of the usual hot water and asked, "What is happening?" She had not yet had any morning morphine and was very alert. Her breath was down to eight breaths per minute (it should have been twelve to sixteen), and her oxygen level was 94 percent and going down.

Finally she had a blowout in her Big Girl Pants but didn't need any clothing changes, just a wash. Her oncologist and also the head of nursing came in. The oncologist said he was going to up her patch to get her off so much IV morphine.

I spoke to the doctor in the hall, and he said she had two to four weeks left. She had a bit of swelling in her right hand and a tiny bit in her ankles. None of this was serious, just a pattern starting.

Barb was on saline IV for hydration and had not had any food that had stayed down in weeks. We gave her a very strong Tylenol for the severe pain in her hips, which meant that the cancer had definitely spread to the bones. Testing was too invasive. Barb said she was tired of fighting, didn't care about how much medicine she got as long as she was out of pain, and just wanted to sleep. My beautiful sister was no longer viable for the most part.

I got up early and went shopping at the purse store down the street, at Barb's insistence. It was good to get out for an hour. Sherry stayed with Barbara, and when I came back and showed her my purchases, Barb was so happy. She still delighted in shopping, even someone else's.

The oncologist came in and watched her being sick. Earlier Barb and I had a talk about how bad she felt. I told her, "Stop telling the doctor that you feel fine and 'better than yesterday' with a big smile. Tell him the truth!"

So she finally did. He seemed shocked, even though Sherry had spoken to him on the phone the evening before, trying to tell him how ill Barb really was. He prodded her stomach to see what was going on and tapped organs, but he was silent. We got the message even though he wasn't talking. He said she was feeling roughly what she should be feeling at this stage. He said she would wake up at times and not know where she was or why.

"Don't be afraid," he said. "Your family is here with you." This was the first such conversation that had taken place. He also said that if the gas got too bad he could try to extract it, but Barbara was not into that!

Part of Barbara's cancer was the overproduction of bile and gas, so we burped her like a baby when she woke up. Whenever she burped, we danced around, clapping and congratulating her. She would try hard at times to make us perform.

The pain doctor came in and changed her neurology medications to stronger ones and also gave us a cream to rub on her back — a topical pain-killer. Sherry gave Barb backrubs regularly and pounded her back to release gas, and Wanchai would rub her legs and feet in the evening.

Sometimes Barb had flashes of imagination, like telling me to turn off the tap drip that was driving her nuts. No, she was not dreaming and no, there was no tap drip. She wanted me to phone people for her and give them messages, often work related. She said that I needed to call the lawyer to check on her immigration status. She had a year-long visa but thought she had to report in every three months. I agreed to everything, trying to ease her mind.

Sherry left to go to Doi Suthep, the beautiful temple up the mountain, by red truck. That is the only thing she still wanted to do. Barbara had had us running for six days while she crossed off her bucket list, and she could bark off orders from a wheelchair or a hospital bed like a pro. She now insisted that Sherry take this trip. I certainly agreed, as it was something not to be missed if you're in Chiang Mai.

Barb gave Sherry some money to look for bird-watching binoculars for Steve for his birthday. Every day, she mentioned that this needed to be done. She also wanted a good Thai bird book for him, so Sherry went out the door with a list of things to do in addition to visiting the temple. Sherry bought a fairly large reclining Buddha image at Doi Suthep for herself as well as some little gift Buddha images that could be put on chains but didn't find the binoculars for Steve.

Barb's readings were coming in normal, except for her oxygen level. She took a nausea pill and went back to sleep. For two hours, she waved her arms in the air as she slept, pointing her fingers, very animated. This was new behavior.

Was Barbara's time drawing near? Would Sherry still be here when the time came? I knew we were losing Barbara, but when? Barb had always kept her hands folded near her body, protective, and today for the first time, she stretched her arms out to the side, welcoming.

Every now and again my Barbara appeared, with her quirky sense of humour. One night after a particularly glorious vomiting session, we got Barb back into bed, and I headed to the bathroom. Sherry said, "Where are you going, Mom?"

And Barb quickly replied, "I hear her escaping out the window."

The amazing thing was that three strong women lived in one room, with that ominous threat always lurking about, yet we laughed, talked, and eagerly supported each other's needs, and the moments ticked by without conflict or ego. We were all changed forever.

Time did pass very quickly, and we were never bored. My friend the iPad was a means of communicating with family and friends back in Canada, and I did a lot of research regarding Barb's illness. Her co-workers e-mailed regularly, and Barb loved it when I read a message from one of her friends. When I was tired of doing research, I read *The Tibetan Book of Living and Dying* by Sogyal Rinpoche (1992), and it was excellent. Barb had given it to me.

Wanchai came in with our dinner and lay down beside Barb, as he did most nights. He just needed to be near her. Sherry and I went for a stroll down the hall, ending up on the leather couch in front of the window by the fountain. We spent a lot of time there when Wanchai and Barb needed time alone. The sound of the water trickling over rocks was soothing, and there wasn't much in our hospital room that felt soothing. After an hour, we went back, and Wanchai kissed Barbara as he was leaving. He whispered to her, "Please don't leave me." This was so hard.

Often on Saturdays, after English school, Art spent the afternoons with us in the hospital. When he asked his dad to bring him for an I-want-to-hug-Barbara visit, we showered her the night before and washed her hair and curled it at her request so she would look pretty. She said this could be the last time he would see her and she wanted him to have a good memory.

The next morning we all slept in. Barb woke at 10:30 a.m., received her meds, and went back to sleep. Wanchai and Art arrived at 11:30. We were just getting ready to cut some breakfast pineapple, so Wanchai did that job for us. Barb asked for some pineapple and ate one tiny piece and drank 1 ounce of Sprite. When Wanchai and Art left, they dropped Sherry off at the mall by the hospital, Kad Suan Kaew, so she could once again look for binoculars for Steve.

Sherry came back from the mall with a great pair of binoculars, but Barb was very disappointed that the binoculars did not cost more. She was thinking more in Canadian prices, I think. Sherry also bought some pants for the boys and a couple of pairs of beautiful shoes for herself. Barb was going in and out of sleep. The staff put Barbara on oxygen when her reading came in at 84 percent.

Later, Wanchai's sister Pum and her two daughters, who were home from university, visited for a while and brought a huge bouquet of two-dozen beautiful red roses. After the visitors left, we three inmates went to sleep.

At 2:00 a.m. I was awakened by Barb calling out, "Rene!" Sher and I got up, as she wanted to sit up but couldn't by herself. She was scared and talking about horses. She didn't know what was wrong — no pain, no nausea, no difficulty breathing. When I felt her back, it was so hot, but her fingers and feet were cold. Sherry called for a nurse to take Barb's temperature, and it was slightly elevated at 101.2°F. The nurse brought her something to take her temperature back down. She went to the toilet but could not stand on her own or manage to sit alone. We got her back into bed, and she smiled.

I said, "Why are you smiling, honey?"

She answered, "There are babies! They are sitting all around me!"

Some of this was caused by lack of oxygen to the brain, as even with oxygen supplement she was only at 94 percent. Her breathing was shallow and irregular but back up to the normal 15 breaths per minute. Barb's red blood cells were no longer able to deliver sufficient oxygen on their own. It was all part of a slow general shutdown. Fluid was starting to gather in her lungs; lately on a couple of occasions, she'd been coughing really deep, noisy coughs.

She was almost comatose all day. Now that she needed an oxygen supplement, I thought that, well, we were headed downhill. But Wanchai came in at 6:00 p.m. and she perked up, sitting on the side of the bed, laughing and joking, kissing and hugging like she wasn't even sick. She was amazing! When Wanchai left, he was so happy, saying, "She all right! She getting better! Yesterday low-low, today high-high!"

After he left, she wanted a shower and clothing change. She slept well all night, except for the coughing. She was actually putting on weight because she was starting to swell, so she looked plumper. We would get perhaps an hour of interaction a day, maybe less. She performed for the doctors daily, saying she felt better and had no issues. They always commented on her beautiful smile.

I climbed into my bed after Barb and Sherry fell asleep, but I stayed awake. My mind simply would not shut down as a thousand thoughts and worries spun around in my head. Sherry would be glad to get back to her family soon. I would still be in purgatory for a while. Barbara wandered in and out of hell.

I knew that I could clean out Barb's things in half a day, and I didn't need to stay for the funeral. I felt so guilty for wishing this was over, but I was getting tired, and the grief at times was overwhelming. The nurses would provide the extra help I would need after Sherry left. They'd had it pretty good up until now. Sher had been here for the roughest stuff, and we felt we had her medications down pat, just adding more as needed. It was like living on the edge of a cliff, never knowing when the edge was going to crumble. This could go on for weeks.

Wanchai continued to be wonderful to me. He was so grateful that I was there and called me "the big bott" (boss). It was a respect thing. He was so afraid I was going to leave with Sherry.

Until Mom died, I hadn't thought much about my own mortality. I practiced the I'm-going-to-live-forever mantra. Suddenly, Mom was gone. Both Barbara and I took her loss very hard, and we both had great difficulty sleeping. I thought I was going to cry forever and grew so tired of the hard ache that gripped my chest like a vice. Sherry watched me in my grief and said that she began to question how she would be able to deal with losing me or her dad. The grief consumed me at times. Bob was patient — and there.

When Mom died, Barbara and I had had the responsibility of liquidating her life. We started with an estate sale, advertising items on the Internet, and had a gigantic garage sale. I priced every item of Mom's, and Barbara priced her own items, as she was moving to Thailand and could go with just four suitcases. She did put together a half a dozen boxes, which I mailed to her later. She took some of her things to her work place, such as dozens of scarves, clothing items, and knick-knacks, to give to her fellow workers.

When one lives to be 89 years old, one accumulates so much. A lot of Mom's things were precious only to her. Every morning, for almost four months, I picked up coffee and a muffin for Barbara and me on the way to Mom's house. We sat at her dining room table and decided what the day would entail. We both did nothing except what was needed to dispose of each item in this very large home and prepare Barbara for her new life. Several truckloads of what could only be called garbage went to the dump. After the garage sale and furniture disposal, when the house was almost empty, we listed the house for sale. It sold fairly quickly, and then Barbara had a date for her permanent move to Thailand. She was taking her dog, Koke, with her.

During this time, Barbara and I grew very close. We had been close in the past, but the bond we forged this time was a forever bond. We shared intimately the loss of our mom and all that was entailed in her passing. We shared the grief.

The grief slowly got better, but it was never gone. After Barb moved to Thailand, she and I e-mailed every day, and often our words were support sessions for each other. We passed the first anniversary of Mom's death, and both of us felt that the worst was now behind us. I did, however, begin to think of my own passing. This had always been a place of fear for me, so I pretended it would never happen. I began to think about it and ask myself all the mortality questions. I had no answers. All these memories and thoughts whirled around when I should have been sleeping.

I finally passed out but woke up in the wee hours again, my mind still racing. Sherry was awake too. We finally went back to sleep around 5:00 a.m. and woke up at 8:00. Barbara remained asleep. Her morning readings at 6:00 a.m. were still not good, but at 10:00, her readings were all normal.

Art and his mom, Noi, came for a visit. She and Barbara were friends despite the language barrier. They used to go shopping together on occasion, and she often visited Barbara at the house. Once Noi said to Barbara in very hesitant words, which she had obviously memorized, "I love Art. You love Art. So I love you."

Art lived with Barb and Wanchai on the weekends, where he had his own room, computer, and television set. His Thai family was two minutes away, so he travelled between his two homes at will. Sometimes after school, he would park his bicycle in the carport at Barb's, get himself a yogurt from the fridge, gobble it down, and then scoot home. His mom did not buy yogurt.

The pain doctor came in very early in the morning. He was fresh out of surgery. Because she was retaining some fluid, Barb told her doctor that her feet looked like the cookie (gingerbread) man's feet.

We had a quiet morning together. Barb was feeling good, so we did some on line banking on her computer, paid her Visa, and answered some emails. She dictated and I typed, as she had not been able to type for a long time. It was just too hard. Sherry took a red truck to Tha Phae Gate to find a bird book to add to the binoculars for Steve's birthday gift from Barb. Not only did she find a book, but she also found our favourite clothing designer and bought three great tops and a hat. Barbara and I had stumbled upon this store years ago and always managed a visit and subsequent purchases when we were in town together. Sherry found the store by accident.

Sherry was leaving shortly for home. She had quickly learned to love Thailand through Barbara's eyes and her life. Sherry knew that she wanted to return soon but under different circumstances. Thailand was magical to her. I already knew that.

When the oncologist came in very late in the day, he prescribed two diuretics to be taken at 8:00 p.m. We would have been up all night! The nurse called the hospital doctor on call, and he agreed that the diuretics could be given in the morning, as this was not a life-threatening situation. That would mean we could sleep at night and deal with the water retention in the morning. Barb did have a good night's sleep. Oxygen levels started to be an issue; Barb needed sufficient oxygen to keep the brain and heart functioning well but not too much, as pancreatic cancer cells flourish in oxygen. It was a balancing act.

The oncologist had also ordered a protein supplement (albumin) and put Barb on an IV diuretic (Lasix), as the pill form diuretic wasn't doing the job. Fluid was collecting in her lungs. Nobody liked that.

Sherry and I had our usual eggs and rice from the bakery. (Two orders were 87 baht, about $2.85, including Sher's Thai tea). When they saw her coming in the door, they simply put together the two orders and handed them to her. Crazy farangs always eat the same thing! At 11:30 a.m. Sher went to the drug store to get some more Big Girl Pants but didn't find what was wanted, so she bought some shoes instead. She shopped like her Auntie Barb.

Barb was suddenly very active, very busy. She tried to work on her computer for a while, deleting some files. The voiding from the diuretic started, coming at 3:15, 4:15, 5:15, 7:15, and 9:30 p.m. It made a huge difference in her feet, ankles, and legs. Barb had had serious pitting edema for a couple of days. She was pretty empty now. A quiet evening ensued with Wanchai coming to visit at 8:00 p.m., with soup for tomorrow.

At 1:00 a.m. I woke up to the sound of Barbara vomiting into her bucket. We had a small container — actually, it was a bucket — and we put a water-proof garbage bag into it so that disposing of the contents was very easy. We put the used bag outside the door, and the cleaning staff would quickly take it away. Barb was sick two or three times a day. She said that she was thinking about the fact that Sherry was leaving, and she started to feel sick. Almost anything triggered her stomach upheaval. This was all normal.

At 8:00 in the morning, we three were up, and Sherry got ready to go to Doi Saket in the tuk-tuk to load up her suitcases. As she packed her things from the hospital, we perched Barbara upright in bed so that her back pain and gas were minimal. She admitted that she was having some hallucinations. There was a white light around Sherry, and there were some strangers in the room.

Before Sher left, Barbara asked her, "Sher, is this as good as I am going to get?" Barb was having some trouble breathing now, as the bottom of her lungs was filling.

Sherry replied, "I think so, Auntie." I joined in the conversation, and we talked about communication after death and about our mom and dad. Mom, we had decided, comes as a rainbow, and Dad comes as sunshine. It was a very loving exchange. Sherry left at 10:00 a.m. for Doi Saket.

For a change, I put Barbara in her wheelchair with a footstool, and she sat in comfort for a half hour or so. She was in always in bed, and a change in position was good. Today she admitted that her breathing was getting tougher. This was the first time for that admission from her.

Before they returned to the hospital that evening, Wanchai took Sherry to our favourite park on the moat. They fed the fish and then had a light snack at the little restaurant inside the park, arriving at Sriphat Hospital at 6:00 p.m. We all (except Barb) had some of the dinner that Wanchai had brought, and just before 9:00 p.m., Sherry and Barbara said goodbye.

They quietly talked, wept, and hugged each other for a very long time. Then there were no words. Barbara bowed her head to Sherry, and she *waid*. Sherry returned the *wai* and bowed her head until their foreheads touched. As their hands in the *wai* position reached to each other, their pinky fingers touched. They now were both crying, and they enveloped each other's hands to make one *wai*.

Barbara said to Sherry, "When you hug your children, your husband, your mother, your father, your brother, your sister-in-law, your niece, or your nephew, know that I am hugging you too." It was very moving. Sherry was saying goodbye for all of us who loved Barbara.

At 9:00 p.m., Wanchai and Sherry left for the airport. Barbara and I cried and cried and held each other for a very long time. "I'll never see her again," Barb said. True. "How do you say goodbye forever?"

At 11:30 p.m., Barb woke up saying, "Rene, what's wrong? There's something wrong!"

I said, "I don't know. Are you in pain?"

"Yes, in my back, but I need to go to the bathroom, too."

She realized that it was the pain that awoke her, and while we were in the bathroom, we heard Sherry's plane taking off, at midnight.

Barb kept saying, "Why am I in so much pain?"

I said, "There goes Sherry's plane!" We could see the runway from our room.

Barb exclaimed, "That's why! I'm feeling the pain of Sherry leaving, hers and mine!" She repeated, "How do you say goodbye forever?"

I had no answer for her. My time and her time to leave forever would come.

Chapter Ten

"Nothing is forever, except change."
—Gautama Buddha

BARBARA and I cried together again, and at 12:30 a.m., Barb was sick. I ordered morphine for her, and she finally went to sleep.

Sherry had been the gofer for the last month, rustling up whatever we needed. Now I was reliant on others such as Wanchai to bring food. I wasn't comfortable leaving Barb alone even for the 10 minutes it took to get something from the bakery across the street, which also sold made-up Thai dinners that were very good. I'd figure it out. Right now the fridge was full of food.

Barb had begun to retain water significantly, so she was on diuretics and I had to measure all liquid in and all liquid out of her body. That was a job in itself. I prepared a chart so that it was easy to track and follow, and I had my daily "meds and occurrences" record. The nurses and doctors looked at my chart when they needed information such as "When did she vomit?" or "How much breakthrough morphine?" I had 14 things that I tracked.

They were worried about congestive heart failure because her lungs were starting to fill a bit. There was no danger yet. She might hold on for a very long time. She was lucid most of the time, and then I caught her making little spit balls out of tissues and shooting them into an imaginary basket, cursing when she missed the shot. Living with her wasn't dull. Barb was truly not ready to give up the good fight.

She said to me, "This might be the best I will be."

People told her, "Get better, get better!" and so for a while, she actually thought she would get better. We did talk again about communication after death. I wouldn't tell her that her time was limited; she did not want to hear that. When she wanted to know something, she would ask. We finally went to sleep.

We woke up at 7:00 the next morning, and I showered. After her 9:30 morphine, Barb went back to sleep. I read for a while and ate a delicious mango. The pain doctor came in at 2:00 p.m. and upped her patch to fifty. When awake, Barb was in charge. I was now doing the work of two, and Barb was busy. True to form, Barbara had me running my tushie off.

"Change this. Why don't we try that? What about this? Would you get me this? Or that? Or more? Or less!" I knew it was coming, and I also knew that one day she would no longer be the director.

She soon slept, exhausted from all the tasks! I cried a lot, every chance I got, but not in front of her, not when she was awake. I didn't want to upset her. I didn't want to get bopped on the head.

I rearranged furniture for her and did anything I could to make her comfortable. We were both trying to get rid of that first day without Sherry.

I was afraid that I wouldn't last the almost three weeks that I had left in Thailand, and how would I ever be able to leave her? I hurt so bad for her pain, her journey, and it was taking a toll on me. Part of the crying was about missing Sherry, missing her laughter, her antics, her help. She'd done so many things, took over so many tasks, and did all the gofer jobs. She was just such a joy. But Sherry and I had vowed that we would do whatever was necessary to make this as easy for Barbara as we could. She would never be alone, and our only objective was her comfort. I now carried the responsibility.

When the doctor came in, he ordered a Fleet enema, as Barb was very worried about a blockage. She knew what that would mean. She argued that she hadn't pooped since we arrived (she had twice) and of course argued about everything that I had written on the chart. I was grateful that I'd had a heads-up on all of this. Most of this behavior could be attributed to the morphine. She'd already had an argumentative personality, so now it was much exaggerated. It would worsen as her drugs became even stronger. I knew better than to take any of it personally. My job was just to love her and do my best to help her as she travelled down this unwanted path. I would have time later to ask questions of the universe.

She wanted Rice Krispies but didn't want the milk from the fridge (too old) and didn't want me to go and buy some, and so she pouted. She finally settled for some peaches, which she threw up, but she did let me know that the custard baby food she had purchased tasted like shit. I didn't offer that again.

I thought that perhaps her bowels had shut down. Her trunk was filling with water, and her legs, feet, and ankles had pitting edema again. Barb slept all afternoon, her patches were changed at 5:00 p.m., and she vomited at 6:00. Barb felt very sick all day.

A Thai lady who Barbara knew well came to visit with flowers, a beautiful pink arrangement of roses, but she upset Barbara by crying. Barb insisted that a sign be put on the door saying, "Family Visitors Only." The next day she asked me to take the sign down. She slept from 9:00 p.m. to 6:00 a.m. I was ready for the feathers at 3:00 in the afternoon. How was I going to manage three weeks of this? Yes, I knew how. One day at a time. I got it.

It was difficult with Sherry gone but not that much more than this whole journey. Barb knew she wasn't going home again. She gave me the white gold earrings that she had bought on our very first trip to Thailand together and the jade Buddha that she wore on a chain. I put the Buddha on my chain and still wear it. It was very symbolic. We talked about that first trip and how it changed our lives forever. Much of my grieving I was doing then, with the thought that it would make it easier later. It didn't.

Wanchai got sick with the flu but still visited nightly wearing a mask. Barb was furious that he was spreading germs all over the room. She told him to "no touch me." He touched her anyway, and then after he left, I washed her legs and hands as well as the room and bathroom with antiseptic soap. If I missed a spot like the fridge door or the phone, she noticed immediately, so I just did it right the first time. She worried about an infection, which of course would be deadly to her.

I was awake at 3:00 a.m., e-mailed Bob, and made out a new record chart. Sleep had become a luxury. I worried about Barb's oxygen level dropping quickly, as that could do brain damage.

Enema day for her was always an exhausting procedure. The doctors weren't concerned about the lack of elimination for five days, but she was so worried about a blockage. In actuality, her bowels may have shut down. Testing for any of these things was just too invasive.

In the morning, a team of nursing assistants took on the task of delivering the Fleet, which was unsuccessful, and Barb insisted that it hadn't been done correctly. She was very intimidating to the two young interns who had been given the task of performing this procedure. They were scared, and she was mad. Finally they called for help, and one of our nurses took over with a new Fleet and managed to eliminate about a tablespoon. This whole process took almost two hours. Barb was very happy, as there was no blockage, but she was then pooped out. The higher patch of Fentanyl along with the morphine IV for breakthrough pain when needed, was working better. She had no breakthrough morphine all day until 9:00 p.m.

But Barbara was full of water. Her feet, ankles, legs, hips, and belly were swollen and tender. How much was in the lungs was a mystery to me. Every time she got up and moved about, she had terrible back pain.

I planned on reading for a while, but if Attila the Hun got some energy, I would be hopping again. It sure did make the day go by quickly, and I fell asleep as soon as my head hit the pillow. I didn't always stay asleep.

Pancreatic cancer has a terrible prognosis. I read that 94 percent of pancreatic patients are deceased within five years of diagnosis. For breast cancer patients, it is 10.8 percent, and for prostate cancer, it is 0.8 percent. This was one tough disease. I'd heard of patients who were diagnosed on Friday and gone the next Tuesday. It just could not be diagnosed in enough time. No wonder doctors shuddered at the term. Barb was almost cancer-pain free at this time, but she still suffered so. Her bones ached, and she had bedsores that were hard to eliminate. Three vomits a day came, in the blink of an eye. So far we had managed to hit the bucket each time, but that would stop soon too, I surmised.

We had visitors coming on occasion, but their obvious shock at Barbara's condition really upset her. Her loss of weight was obvious, and she was hooked up to all kinds of machinery. Barb said, "What do they think, that I'm up here eating bonbons and watching reruns of *M*A*S*H** with full make-up on?"

Some people were just curious. You know, how vehicles slow down beside a car accident in the hopes of seeing something horrific. They were used to seeing the red-headed spitfire, zooming around, full of life and vitality, laughing and joking and smiling that gorgeous smile. This was tough on everyone.

With Sherry gone, I was left to care for Barb's personal needs, and the medical staff tended to her medical needs. Her doctors visited daily and monitored her well-being. Little pain and as much comfort as possible was the operative modality. Nurses couldn't do the things that Sherry and I did for Barbara, and now I alone was responsible.

I got her ice chips, I put a cold cloth on her forehead, I combed her hair, I cut her fingernails, and I brought her water or pop or juice. I held the bucket while she vomited and then helped her brush her teeth. I assisted her to the toilet, lifting her on and off. I changed her clothing, listened to her fears, shared her memories. We had been a personal team of three; now we were down to two. This was an act of love, not a chore. It was an honour to share this path with her, just as my loving daughter Sherry did with our mother and as Elizabeth, my dear friend, did with her husband. I was beginning to understand commitment and empowerment on a different level.

My family was worried about me and how I was coping, but I think I did convince them that I was fine and that I would be fine. I was in Chiang Mai to be with my sister constantly so that she wasn't without compassionate family who loved her unconditionally. Wanchai couldn't be with her all day and night. His grief was overwhelming, and he was living in a fog.

I felt tremendous sadness, but I also felt joy. I cried, but I also laughed. Barbara was so grateful for my presence, with so little that she could do for herself. How helpless she must have felt, always able to care for herself in the past, and now she walked with an IV pole — when she could walk — and she wore diapers. This proud, sensitive woman was reduced to infant-type needs, and yet she carried on, smiling bravely. She never complained about her misfortune, and she could still send me into gales of laughter. I was so grateful to be there with her. Few people are ever given such an opportunity. And so I plugged away, at Sriphat Hospital for the unintentionally terminal.

Barbara was very shaky and disoriented. This was the first time that had happened in the morning to this extent. Yet her sense of humour remained, even though the brain was struggling with reality. She produced stomach gas like a methane swamp. Whenever she belched, I would say, "Hurrah!" Or clap my hands. She let out a luscious belch. I exclaimed, "Nice!"

She replied, "Yeah, if you are a moose!"

A bit later I asked how she was feeling, and she said, "Aww wight! That was Ewmer Fudd."

See what I mean? She was a pistol. But then, on the toilet, she sprayed herself before she voided, put no toothpaste on her toothbrush but still brushed her teeth, and then dried her hands on toilet paper and threw it on the floor when she was finished. Barb had been a meticulously tidy person who was very structured. Everything was all mixed up.

She couldn't talk this morning or maybe concentrate. There was no answering of questions; she just gave a nod or a shake. This all could change as the morning moved on.

Once, she started to smile, eyes closed. I asked her what she was thinking, and she said, "I'm at a wedding, and all the girls are so pretty, but everyone is wearing gum boots." She smiled her glorious smile.

Barb was having some difficulty breathing but only when lying down, so I perched her up again like a little cockatoo. She loved that analogy and would giggle as she said, "Barbie wants a cracker!" She didn't. It was just funny to her to say it.

Her legs were outstretched so as not to let gravity feed the edema. Her vomit cycle was now three a day, but last night was rough, as she couldn't breathe. Usually she did her job, and then I did mine. But last night she was very frightened. She didn't know why.

The very nice medical student from the U.S. dropped in again while Barb was asleep, but she stayed for an hour. I found making idle conversation very tiring under the circumstances. I didn't know her and would never see her again, so to me it was a waste of time. I knew she was lonely and for some reason she felt comfortable with us. I have always been a great talker, so this was an unusual feeling for me. I just needed to be alone with my sister.

After Barb woke up, we went out onto the deck, and she sat with her head on the rail. The pain doctor came in to check on her, and as soon as Barb saw him, she grabbed my yogurt out of my hand and ate what was left. It was so important to her that she give the right impression. This time, the impression she needed to deliver was that she was eating. The bad news was that she wanted to know exactly what he'd said about her eating and drinking. He'd said nothing about that subject, but when I relayed that information to her, she insisted that I was withholding. I finally just said that I didn't hear him, that maybe I was off the balcony then. (I never went off the balcony.) She was happy with that. There was lots of this going on. I put her back to bed.

She said to me or to herself, "I need to eat more and drink more." And then she passed out.

I slept only four or five hours a night. I had no problem going down, but I didn't get back to sleep if I woke up for any reason. I kept thinking about her short time left. Quick naps in the daytime when she was sleeping were difficult.

Wanchai brought me soup for dinner, and when he was here, I popped down to the 7-Eleven for some things. It was good to get out for a few minutes.

The diuretics were working to a degree, but Barb's trunk was really full. I had to cut the legs on her Big Girl Pants as well as the back waist. Her left hand was swelling (the IV was in her left arm), but I didn't know where that would take us. Maybe we would be looking at an arm switch for the IV.

She couldn't make it to or from the bathroom without holding onto the pole, the counter, and then the bed. She was shaking badly, right hand especially, and she was trying hard to keep her oxygen on, which stayed around 90 percent. It dropped very quickly if it was taken off, like when she took a bathroom break.

She planned a shopping trip for us to the mall. "Rene, how will we deal with a vomit?" she asked.

"I don't know. What do you think?"

"I know!" she said. "We will go right after I vomit."

Within two minutes, she had forgotten about the shopping trip.

She wanted to find a wheelchair that had an IV pole attachment and a "legs straight out attachment" so that her edema wouldn't be fed by her legs hanging down when we went on these magical excursions. Luckily, she didn't remember her own plans, and if she did, she couldn't make it to the elevator without me. I was getting good at redirecting.

She said, "I'm just like a baby now."

I said, "Yep, and you are my baby."

Mom came one night: I looked out the window around 7:00 p.m. Over the umbrella-like canopy of trees that were on the left of the balcony, close in, like trees on the Serengeti, was the most beautiful rainbow. It filled the sky and ended in those trees. I felt like I could reach out and touch it. A full range of colour, mauve, blue, green, yellow, orange, and red in a brilliance that I had never seen before, danced across the sky, and another duller rainbow was beside it. The large rainbow was so bright and so close. It was Mom. It made Barbara happy that Mom was watching us.

I was still measuring liquids that no one cared about, so I just ran totals. Mornings were good, and I tried to keep Barb's feet up. She often liked to be propped up with her legs dangling over the edge of the bed, but this caused her legs and feet to swell almost immediately.

I needed to get through the next two weeks. I hoped to return home to Vancouver Island then, unless it was evident and guaranteed that a day or two would tell the tale. This could be over tonight or go on for another month. I was becoming more and more exhausted, and I wasn't the one with the hourglass countdown.

Barbara no longer had much quality of life, and I told the pain doctor, "No heroic measures," when he asked. Wanchai, Barbara, and I had discussed all of this, and Barb didn't want to be resuscitated, should she go into heart failure.

I said to the doctor, "I think soon."

He said, "Yes, soon." But what was soon? *Mai pen rai.* Never mind.

Barb was hallucinating a lot, and we laughed about what she imagined. She saw a baby wearing a toque across the way on the balcony of the next building, and three or four toques were dancing on the rail beside the baby. Another time, she reached for her bucket and didn't know which one to grab. There were two. Then one disappeared. She loved it when the children and babies appeared, and they appeared often. Her doctor told us to talk about her hallucinations in order to take away any fear factor. She told the nurse that her legs were swollen because she had been out dancing all night. I'm sure she had been.

Barb and I woke up at 7:00 a.m., as the nurses did not wake us up at the normal 6:00 a.m. They saw that we were sleeping and held off on the blood pressure measurements. Barb slept most of the day. Art arrived at 5:00 p.m. with a new game and a "creature" to build, which he did. Art was very loving and adored Barbara so much. We had dinner together. Wanchai picked Art up at 10:00 to take him home.

Barb's feet and knees were now mottled purple — a sign of the beginning of congestive heart failure. There was some mottling in her legs, but that had been going on for a while. She kept saying, "I'm so tired." She just wanted to sleep. She snored loudly with some gurgling, and her breath was shallow, rising from her abdomen, not her chest.

Last night we'd talked about death, so I asked her if she was afraid, and she said she wasn't. We talked about communication after death and agreed that only the body dies; the memories and the love remain forever. She seemed very calm about it all. This was becoming a common topic of discussion.

At 2:00 a.m. Barb was calling me because she'd had a nightmare. She thought she had died and couldn't wake me up. Bells kept ringing three times on her right side, and she thought that the nurses were trying to call her. We went to the bathroom, and she was very weak and unsteady on her swollen feet.

I put her back to bed and crawled in with her, holding her until she fell asleep, and then went into my own bed at 4:00 a.m. I woke at 7:00, and Barb was sitting up, talking to no one.

She asked for things such as oranges but then didn't want them. She wanted Jell-O but then wouldn't touch it because "what you gave me is a solid, and Jell-O is a liquid." There was an imaginary man in the room, but she wasn't afraid of him. However, Barb wasn't always confused. She talked about things that didn't make sense, but believe me — she could snap out of it in a heartbeat if a doctor came in.

Art and his mom visited for a half an hour, and Barb slept through the visit. It broke my heart when Art said to Barb, "I'll see you next Saturday." He adored her so. He referred to her as his "Canada mother." Barbara told me that she in no way saw herself as Art's mother; he already had a wonderful mother. But Art and Barb were very close.

While they were visiting, I scooted out for some food. I went to the little vendor on the street for some chicken on a stick. It looked just like the chicken Sherry had brought us one day.

"Guy?" I asked. *Guy* is chicken. *Moo* is pork. *"Guy?"* I asked again.

"Yes, *moo!*" the vendor replied.

"*Guy* later?" I asked.

"No *guy* later. *Mooo.*" It was *moo.* So we had eaten pork. No wonder they were howling at Sherry. We didn't eat pork unless we thought it was chicken. So I got an angel hair pasta from the bakery instead.

The nurses could still put meds into the port in Barbara's arm by injection, but there was no pole. Barb's belly was large now, and her hand was swollen. Her hands and feet were cold. Hands weren't yet blue at the nail bed. She often talked gibberish.

"Bob has two cell phones. One is for water, and one is for food. Don't get the numbers mixed up. Did you know that?"

"Why is the measuring urinal named 'Mom'? Is it only for her to use?" There was no label on the urinal measurer.

These conversations took place on the way to the bathroom. I had to lift her off the bed and on and off the toilet totally now. She had no strength. I was very careful to lift with my legs and trunk, not my back only. I thought, "I have lost my sister." There seemed to be little life. Just sleep, vomit, pee, sleep.

When the oncologist came in, he decided to cut her IV nourishment down to one day on and one day off to give her veins a rest. I read and finished my lunch while he was there, trying to stay out of their interaction. One was lying, and the other was pretending to believe the lies.

"How do you feel today?"

"I feel wonderful. I'm all right!"

"That's good. Does this hurt?"

"No, that's okay."

"Good. I'll see you tomorrow."

"Yes, I'll see you tomorrow."

I kept my nose in my book. The oncologist didn't control her pain medications and so was completely out of the picture, but Barb still liked his daily visits.

I didn't know what was keeping her going. She had consumed so little food for weeks, even months. Her cancer — in addition to the tumor in the pancreas — was in her spleen, liver, lungs, lymph nodes, abdominal wall, and bones. It had migrated to her brain as well. She was so tough. Tough *soi* dogs, tough Thai kids, tough Barbara.

In the middle of the night, Barb was up and wandering about the room, pushing her wheelchair. There was no pole, as she was off the IV for 24 hours.

She accepted the vomiting now as part of the day. She would wake up with a start, sit for a few minutes, and then say, "I'm going to be sick." I would grab the bucket, hold it for her, give her tissues, and clean her up — bag out the door, new bag, teeth brushed, just like clockwork.

Art's Mom came for a visit, so I went to the fountain area to give her some time with Barb. They were holding hands when I left. I noticed that to the left of Kad Suan Kaew was a crematorium and that one of the two smoke stacks was belching white smoke, the first sign of a cremation. Then it turned opaque so you couldn't see the crematorium. I wished I could get out so that I could go and watch, but I wouldn't leave Barb. It was hard enough to go for ten minutes.

The staff was actually talking about sending her home. At least, that was what one of the nurses said. Was there some plan of which we were unaware? Because she did not want to know how long she had, was the oncologist just going to release her and then readmit her? She was on hydration IV and oxygen. Her breakthrough morphine and her anti-nausea medication were given by IV due to her vomiting. There was no IV at home. Did the doctor want her to go home to die and just couldn't say those words? Barb had a policy of "no secrets," so I was not to talk privately to the doctors, nor was Wanchai. I got that. Once when I left with the doctor, she immediately said, "Where are you going? Talk in here so I can hear." But the biggest concern of all had to be kept a secret because she didn't want to know how long she had left.

Two weeks ago, I had been told she had two to four weeks. So was Barb getting the idea that she would get better at home? Right now she was sleeping all day and night, except for vomiting and bathroom. She couldn't get off the bed or on it, nor could she get on or off the toilet, and she walked to the bathroom holding her IV pole and using counters and walls, with me behind to steady her and grab her if she started to go down. She was swollen from the waist down, and the bottoms of her feet were mottled purple.

When I spoke to Wanchai, he said he hadn't spoken to the oncologist about her going home, but the nurses said they were concerned about her becoming addicted to morphine. It's the same conundrum the world over: Don't let the patient get addicted to morphine, even though she's going to die in two weeks.

What we didn't know was that the oncologist had actually taken Barb off the IV morphine and put her on the less potent oral one. They had taken her off the sleeping pills because the "new" red-and-white pill that she'd started over a week ago was also a sleeping pill. She was still on the IV nourishment. They were doing all this so that she would not be IV-dependent and could go home in a week or two. This was from the oncologist, according to the nurses. He said she was getting much better.

At home, we would have portable oxygen, the patch, liquid morphine, no drip, and whatever anti-nausea we could get that was taken orally. Maybe that would be for the best if it happened. She wouldn't last long without the additional support.

She still insisted on eating something on occasion, and then she threw it up an hour later, along with any meds she has taken. Last night she had one of Art's octopus balls. Up it came. Tonight she was showing off for Wanchai, and she had him make freshly squeezed orange juice out of some fresh oranges. She had a piece of sticky rice with sauce and some chicken, which didn't even stay down an hour. Wanchai hadn't seen her throw up before.

She had fresh oranges in the fridge, and I'd previously had to get her orange pop, but then she wanted orange juice. I kept reminding myself that she now had brain damage and this explained the behavior. We tried to give her whatever she wanted.

That night, she had no sleeping pills, and I had a big fight with the nurses about morphine. I got the IV morphine at 10:00 p.m. finally but no sleeping pills. At midnight I called the nurse in to deal with a crying Barb, and the nurse phoned a doctor and got an order for sleeping pills.

Barb kept saying in front of the nurse "Why am I not sleeping?"

I kept saying, "They took your sleeping pills away."

"But why would they do that to me?"

So she and I went to sleep just after midnight. The old order had been cancelled but the new order wasn't recorded. This was a slip-up. Nurses wouldn't give medications without a written order. The doctor deserved to be awakened, I thought resentfully (I would have to make merit for that).

Barb was up at 4:00 a.m., sitting on the edge of her bed and babbling for ages, and then got up and pushed her IV pole around. The intravenous bag ran out at 5:00, and I called a nurse to remove it. She would have no IV pole this day. Well, freedom at last! She spent the next two hours pushing her wheelchair around, walking with the three-footed walker, going in and out of the bathroom. I went in to check on her, and I found her sitting and standing repeatedly. She told me she was practicing going to the bathroom alone. She began walking about the room using the three-footed cane and was wandering, pushing her chair. Her legs were very swollen and hard. She seemed frantic.

"I am practicing getting up and down by myself," she said to no one. I just stayed in bed and watched her. I tried to get her to go to bed, but nope.

Then at 8:00 a.m., she turned on the shower and announced she was washing her hair with or without me. She hadn't asked me to wash her hair. I quickly found a plastic bag, and a nurse waterproofed her port. I locked the door, and in we went onto the shower chair. I washed her, dried her, dressed her, and put her hair in rollers, and then her back pain kicked in. I asked for morphine and they brought it, injecting it into the IV without a word from me. No arguing from the nurses. Just relief.

I changed the bed to freshen it and put her into it after a ridiculous confrontation where she was in the wheelchair and insisted that I had to put my left foot between her legs to lift her up. I said, "I can't, Barb. I am right-handed and have to have my right foot there to use my right side as leverage."

"No, you have to use your left foot. I'm a nurse. That is the only way to do it."

I knew I couldn't. She was now 55 kilos due to water retention. The only way she would let me put my right foot between hers was from the other side of the bed, so I had to wheel her around to the other side. Then I could get her up, right foot between hers, and then place her down on the bed. She always had been stubborn and headstrong, but then, I knew that; I'd known and loved her for 65 years.

Once in bed, she became angry that I had spread my underwear all over the floor, and why did I make such a mess? There was nothing on the floor. Her hallucination even showed her the colours of the underwear. We talked about her hallucination, which seemed to puzzle her, but she immediately forgot what had just happened, as she was losing most short-term memory quickly.

Finally she went to sleep, sitting up now because she coughed if she was flat, and I went down and paid the hospital bill. She was exhausted and slept through my absence. A nurse stayed with her.

The oncologist came in, and everything was going back to how it was, with the addition of an ultrasound in the afternoon to see what was going on in her tummy area. If there was too much fluid, they could drain some extra fluid off.

In two more weeks, I thought, Barb would have little awareness of what was going on around her. I really felt like I had weathered the worst part of her illness with her. Wanchai and I talked that night about how wonderful the last month had been. If she was still here when I left, I would have to let that go. It would appear that she could go on like this for many, many weeks, but I needed to go home in two weeks.

Barb didn't remember her last medication, her last vomit, or her last request for something like orange juice, which Wanchai would dutifully bring. He did everything he could to please her, as did I. It was the least we could do.

Tick-tock.

Chapter Eleven

We are dancing as fast as we can.

—Barbara

DOCTORS and nurses asked Barbara questions for which she just made up answers. I stayed out of it. I no longer measured her water in and out. I had done it for over a week, and the doctors and nurses had checked the numbers the first day only. I asked if I could stop, and they said no, and then Barb made a big fuss about how they would check the totals to see how the retention was going.

Doing these measurements was so hard for us. I had to lift her out of bed, help her to the bathroom, lift her onto the toilet that I had put the bedpan onto, wait for the pee, lift her up, remove the bedpan, put her back down to clean herself, lift her back up, and move her pole to the doorway. She would wash her hands, and then I'd help her to bed and lift her back onto the bed. She had pitting edema, so she got huge dents from the bedpan, and it hurt her. Then I measured the urine by pouring it into a urinal and recorded the findings. Finally, I would wash the urinal and bedpan. The first day she was on Lasix she went seven times. It was great to have a day with no IV pole to drag or push.

The pain doctor came in and in his jovial manner said, "Here comes the needle guy. Do you want the sharp one or the dull one?" He put in a new IV port into her right arm, and at 4:00 p.m., we went off to the ultrasound.

Barb said she wanted to put on full makeup to go to the ultrasound but simply drew circles around her eyes with eyeliner. I didn't interfere, but she did ask me to put her lipstick on, which I did. She was slurring her words and making faces, sticking out her tongue. The drugs were having some very tough side effects now. I still had two weeks to go, and it was getting tougher and tougher.

The ultrasound results showed that there was very little acid in the stomach, so no needle extraction.

We went to sleep at 9:00 p.m., both exhausted, but I was up at 1:00 a.m. when I realized that Barb was in the bathroom alone. She vomited while in the bathroom, and then she went back to bed. Up again in an hour to pee — none came — and then back to bed. She was asleep by 3:00, but I was now awake for the night. At 5:00 I showered and got dressed.

I didn't know how Wanchai was going to manage after I was gone, and I didn't know how I was going to deal with the guilt of leaving her. I knew I had done a lot (not even counting what Sherry did), but it was time for me to get my life back in order.

As long as she passed while I was still in Chiang Mai, it would be fine. I didn't need to be here for the funeral, which would last a week before the cremation. She made very little sense, saw things, was totally confused, and had hallucinations. But she knew me, Wanchai, and Art, and she knew where she was and why.

A lot could change in two weeks, I knew. I would just have to take it as it came. I couldn't believe I had been living in a hospital room for over a month. I had gone out maybe three times to run across the street to the store and for one little purse shopping spree. It was going to get really bad as leaving got closer. Wanchai wanted me to stay forever, and Barb didn't remember that I was leaving soon.

The doctor was in early in the morning, and he basically said there was nothing more that could be done except control pain. His words were, "Just keep her comfortable." Funny, how I'd known that a month ago, and I didn't have a medical degree. It was like doctors always tried to give the illusion of hope (whatever that was), and that was their mandate, I'm sure. *Do no harm.*

Barb heard his words, and she understood. Her eyes got big, and she looked at me as if to say, "Change this!" She had always known intellectually what the prognosis was, but she thought she had more time.

One of the nurses said, "We have to get you off the IV because when you go home, there is no IV. You have to take everything orally."

I was screaming inside, "When you go home!" But Barb, I'm sure, thought she had bought some time. Somehow.

I was at the point that I understood why people wanted loved ones to have their anguish over. She had little life and had lost whatever joy there was in the weeks before. I'd had her on the balcony in her wheelchair in the morning, and she had looked at the view, closed her eyes, and hung her head forward. After a while, I said, "Can you hear the birds?"

"Yes." But her body language stayed the same.

"Do you want to go back in now?"

"Yes."

"Do you have pain?"

"Yes."

"Should I get your morphine for you?"

"Yes."

Her eyes were glassy, and she talked about the things she saw, asking questions like, "Why is that boat here?"

I had to tell her what to do in the bathroom in the right order. I spoke very gently to her. "Pee first, honey. Okay, now use the spray."

She often said, "I'm so confused."

She had slid a lot since Sherry left. But all her organs just kept working. Days were tough when we'd had little sleep.

"How are you this morning?" I asked her when I woke up and saw her.

She responded, "Fine, as soon as I see you." My heart was breaking yet again. While Barb was getting her morphine at 10:30 a.m. she asked once more why the boat was outside near the balcony. I said I would try to find out. She often saw this boat.

We had a quiet afternoon, and she slept a lot. Wanchai came in at 5:00 p.m., put on a lovely Celine Dion tape, and gave Barb a full body massage. She smiled a lot, and he left around 8:00 p.m.

I prepared her for bed, and she took her sleep medications, but it was a rough night. She was up to go to the bathroom seven or eight times. She sat, she wandered, and I was up with her. I was afraid of her falling. She just would not sleep. Her focus was the bathroom.

When she took off her oxygen to get up, she somehow separated a connection and kept saying, "No air! No air!" I called a nurse, and we checked everything and finally got it running again. I went back to bed, and in no time Barb was shuffling to the bathroom. Again.

She had a strong painkiller for neuralgia (nerve pain) that was also a sleep aid, two sleeping pills, and a breakthrough morphine dose, and still she was up all night. In the morning, she didn't remember any of it, including vomiting. So at 8:00 a.m., she finally passed out, and I was like a zombie.

After showering, I could hear Barb talking, so I scurried out to see who was there, but it was just her, talking in her sleep with nary a care. She'd just had her anti-nausea, and I just downed a bottle of water. I told the people at the nursing station that I would be back in half an hour, and would they please check on Barb? I didn't want her to wake up and find herself alone. She was fearful of so many things now. I wouldn't add to her angst if I could help it. I scooted to the store.

Wanchai was so faithful in spending time with her. I knew he loved her dearly, and he stayed for a long time every evening. So the days moved on. People in and out, keep Barb comfortable, read, use the iPad. I sometimes sat outside on the sundeck, high above the treetops, just enjoying the warmth and the beauty of Chiang Mai.

My plans remained to go home on July 14, and I was feeling better about that. I thought Barb would not miss me, as she would be pretty out of it then. It would be okay. The thought of her crying and begging me not to go just killed me, but I didn't think that would happen. She was lucid less and less. I asked what she was thinking, and she said, "I don't think about anything anymore."

She often said, "I don't care." But she still was so frightened when they had to change her port to the other arm. The anesthesiologist did it, and she was fine, but she held onto my hand, and there was fear in her eyes. The change didn't cause pain, of course. The other arm still looked good, as phlebitis hadn't set in.

I had some bad moments or hours, but I knew I would pull through. Lack of sleep was now an issue for me, but that too would be rectified. Nothing was permanent. Was I thinking like a Buddhist? There were times when

Barb wanted to eat, not because she was hungry but because eating would make her well, and then she could go home and get on with her life.

Barb had all of the symptoms of the end of life, but not one of them was severe enough to put her over the edge. She was barely coherent now, spoke slowly and very little, and could not answer questions. Her quality of life was minimal, and I disliked saying that, as there were always good moments. I keep hoping that her lungs would just stop working and put her quietly out of this, but as the doctor said, her organs were in very good shape, and she was strong-willed. Her abdomen was filled with cancer, but nothing had taken down an organ yet. Her lungs were filling with liquid, and she coughed and hacked, but her breath remained strong. Her blood pressure was normal, as were her pulse and body temperature. She wasn't going anywhere yet. What an unbelievably strong woman! My sister!

Wanchai was a wreck. He still asked if she was going to get better soon. Art was just devastated, as was the rest of the family. Wanchai continued to come every night and cry. Barbara simply accepted his reaction. She told me right at the beginning that it would be so difficult for him, and that was why she asked me to clear her personal items from the bedroom. The only one accepting all of this was Barbara.

I had Barb's personal affairs pretty much together, and the rest I could gather fairly quickly. If she died and gave me a day, I could have everything done except for the death certificate.

I told Wanchai that I was leaving on the 14th but wasn't sure if he understood or accepted what I was saying. He was in a daze. I thought that by the time I left, she would be almost comatose and so my absence would have no meaning for her. I could live with that. She was so confused and disoriented, and I knew it would get much worse over the next week and a half. Then the nurses would have to step up. There had been little bedside care for them to do up to now.

Barb's shoulder was just skin and bone, but then her legs were so swollen. Last night Wanchai gave her a very gentle body massage for a very long time and spent a long time on her legs and feet. When he went to leave, she said, "Rene, will you rub my legs? Nobody rubs my legs." Wanchai was devastated. She was awake the whole time, just not aware. She had no memory of the lovely massage, although she'd enjoyed it while it was happening.

He told her that the TV in the bedroom was not working, and she told him to get it fixed before she came home. He looked at me with wide eyes and a smile and said, "She coming home?" You can see how confusing it was for everyone. I was not sure that Barb always knew who I was now, but she always knew Wanchai.

Barb was very uncommunicative the next day. She gave only one-word answers. I wondered if this was how it would be, going forward. She was able to fall asleep by 11:00 a.m. after the nurses brought morphine, and when she woke up she was very cold, teeth chattering. I covered her heavily. The pain doctor came in and said to her, "Your hands are cold. Put them in the microwave. Two minutes." He always managed to get a smile out of her.

She had slept most of the day but had a lot of back pain. He gave me a topical salve for her hips (cancer in the bones), and he also said that lack of sleep would cause additional back pain.

At 5:00 in the morning, I was out on the deck as the city was awakening. Instead of the muted sounds of early traffic, all I could hear was the songs of birds. All different bird melodies were coming from all around. Here on the 14th floor, I overlooked so many groves of trees as well as the city, and it was truly beautiful. A few early morning vending vehicles were visible, the kind that was a modified bike with a sidecar. They had to be ready for the breakfast crowd.

I had become used to eating chicken on a stick for breakfast or whatever was left over from last night. Wanchai kept a steady array of food choices coming, like spicy Thai chicken soup. He brought a couple of days' worth at a time, along with the never-ending ripe fruit. I would love to have this at home in Canada. Fruit ripened in transit just isn't the same.

I ordered Barb's morphine and anti-nausea, as her first words were "morphine now," and then she lapsed back into where ever she went. She suddenly would ask me (or whoever she thought I was) a question out of the blue, perhaps part of a dream or hallucination. Whatever I answered satisfied her, and so began another day. Days seemed to go by so quickly, and I was never bored. I am not the type to get bored, anyway.

The head of nursing here at Chiang Mai University Sriphat Hospital came in. She visited us a couple of times a week. She was 65, bilingual, a little bitty thing who worked twelve-hour days and then went to the gym before she went home. She was an inspiration. Her nurses adored her, and she ran a tight ship. They say the doctors feared her. Barb remained unresponsive during the visit, but I cried.

I changed Barb's bed position regularly so that she got variety. She used to be very fussy about her placement of pillows under her back, as it was so sensitive to pain, but now anything would do. She did wake up to go to the bathroom, but she could hardly walk. Unless things changed soon, the nurses would have to put in a catheter. All her organs continued to function perfectly except maybe her bowels. They might have been blocked. But then, not much went in, and the intestines were 35 feet long and could hold a lot of stuff.

Her doctors agreed that by the time I left, she probably wouldn't know I was gone. That made me feel better. They knew how upset I was about leaving her. She refused to discuss anything about her dying. Death discussions were very general in nature; this was what she wanted. She knew Wanchai would do the funeral, and that was enough. She told him what kind of casket she wanted, and she knew enough about Northern Thai services; having attended many in the village, she understood what Wanchai would arrange. Now she couldn't even talk. This could change, of course, and she might be Chatty Cathy by tomorrow. She kept fooling us all.

All the nursing staff seemed different now. It was as if they all knew something that we didn't. Barb had slept almost continuously for 20 hours.

Wanchai came at 6:30 p.m., took her to the bathroom, and then, when he lay beside her, she nestled her head in the crook of his arm.

Barbara whispered to him, "Don't cry. Don't cry."

Wanchai whispered to her, "Don't die. Don't die." I left them alone.

It was a broken sleep for me that night, as Barb had a really bad night. She was up to go to the bathroom several times, coughing badly. She kept trying to get up but couldn't walk or stand. She moved so much that she slid to the bottom of the bed and partially off the end, and I couldn't lift her back up. I called for help, and two tiny Thai nursing assistants managed to move her up a bit. She was now weighty and hard to move. Barbara was very determined during the night and continually said, "I'm getting up. Help me," as she thrashed about, but she couldn't stand alone. She pulled her air off. I couldn't help her.

At 5:00 a.m. or so, she finally curled up on her right side and went to sleep, legs drawn up. Usually she got vertigo immediately on her side, but this time she didn't. I slept too.

The head nurse came in and spoke to me, saying that the following would occur when death was getting close:

1. Her oxygen level would drop.
2. Her blood pressure would drop.
3. Her skin would become cool.
4. There would be breathing issues — gasping.
5. All urination would stop.

We were all concerned that the end could be near. I wondered if we should be taking her home. We could use portable oxygen and diapers, the same as at the hospital, but no IV drip, and her oral meds might not stay down. We couldn't administer through a port, as was being done now.

What to do? What to do?

Two nurses came in to move her back up to the head of the bed using the draw sheet — a slick maneuver — and I moved the pillows. They put an additional draw sheet beneath her, so there would be two sheets with which to work. Barb didn't awaken through all of this. She was exhausted.

Her pain doctor arrived at 8:00 a.m. He decided to put Barb on a new sleep/pain medication in the form of a drip.

On Tuesday, Barb was coherent. On Wednesday, she was failing. On Thursday, she was in the toaster. And by Friday, she was toast.

I went to the store for ten minutes to get lunch and some pastries. I always informed the staff that I would be gone for a few minutes. Sometimes one of our cleaners would sit with her while I was gone. Barb slept all day. I cleaned up the last of the flower bouquets (I didn't like dying flowers in a hospital room) and tidied up the room. A nurse came in and cleaned Barb's eyes and realized that Barb was running a temperature, so she called for help, and the two nurses wiped Barb with a cool cloth to bring her temperature down. Barb was very upset with this action. Perhaps it was uncomfortable, or perhaps she didn't want strangers handling her at that time. I held her hand and tried to soothe her.

She was now wearing Big Girl Pants all the time, as she couldn't get to the bathroom. A catheter would be far too invasive for her tender abdominal area, and using a bedpan would cause pain as well. Her bladder may have shut down. Barb wouldn't even take water with a straw. It might have been hard for her to swallow. She was looking really rough, and I wondered how much longer she could hold on, but with her strong constitution, it could be for a long time. It was twelve hours before she needed extra morphine at 3:00 p.m.

Her doctor ordered anti-anxiety/pain/sleep medication for bedtime, and I hoped she could take it, because we both needed a good night's sleep. I certainly did. Days were easy, as I was awake, but nights were difficult. I hated to go to sleep in case she needed me. What if I didn't wake up? Although Barb didn't remember Wanchai's visit yesterday, she often called out his name when she needed some help at night.

At 5:00 p.m., she needed to void, and because she couldn't walk, she needed to use her Big Girl Pants. I really had to have my act together to persuade her that it was okay. She kept saying, "I can't, I can't!" but she knew who I was and trusted that it was all right, finally. I had help from a nurse assistant; we removed the old ones, got her washed up, and put new ones on in less time than it would have taken to get Barb to the bathroom when she could walk. This was slick! Loved the Big Girl Pants!

Shortly after Wanchai came in at 8:00 p.m., Barb projectile vomited on the floor, the bed, and all over herself. I called in the team, and they removed her from the bed, stripped her, washed her, and dressed her while others took the bed apart and redid it and housekeeping washed and disinfected the floor. What a fabulous team! This too was done in record time with little discomfort to Barbara. Wanchai had never seen the team in action, and he was impressed.

The family came in to visit at 9:00 p.m., but Barb was unresponsive, as she was exhausted. One of Wanchai's nieces told me that Barb shouldn't be taking morphine, that it was very bad for her, and there were other herbal things that they could get that would cure cancer. There was a doctor in Bangkok who cured cancer if we could get Barbara there, she said. They'd seen it on the Internet. They all just wanted to help and, like me, felt so helpless. Everyone was grasping at straws, trying to make this all go away. They left at 10:00 p.m. This was far too late for a visit, as Barb usually was asleep after her meds at 9:00.

I tucked Barb in, told her that I loved her, as usual, and dragged myself to my couch. I didn't even think about whether I could sleep. I just did.

Chapter Twelve

"Death ends a life, not a relationship"
—Mitch Albom, *Tuesdays with Morrie*

TWICE a week, volunteers brought in a fresh red rose in a bud vase for the table. They sprayed the flower with water, so the rose wore what looked like fresh dew. That fresh fragrant rose typified the care that Barb received in this hospital.

I felt like we were in the final throes with Barb. She was going to take a combo pain/sleeping IV that night with the hopes that it would keep her asleep and not agitated, as she had been last night.

She didn't recognize me with her blank eyes, which opened for only a few seconds. Wanchai stayed with her for an hour last night, but she looked asleep. Today she was noisy and restless.

The doctors said the cancer had gone to the frontal lobe, causing the agitation. It was very common. She was not unconscious.

I washed her face. Her eyes were both weeping, so I called the nurse and found that Barb was running a fever. I thought it might have been pneumonia, which would take her fast. Something had to take her: heart attack, congestive heart failure, pneumonia, stroke, or starvation. I was so hoping that she would go quickly, but as in the past, she had rallied. She had done it at least four times in the last month. She was a lioness.

Somehow today was different. Barbara said she could see me, but I'm not sure she could. She was not moving at all now, all day. The next day would be very interesting, as she would either slide more or do her fantabulous rally.

What a process this was! But I was so glad she knew me today, as she may not recognize me tomorrow. Finally we both slept.

I woke up in the middle of the night for no reason. Barb was sleeping, and I began to listen to her breathe. In, out. In, out. I could feel myself panic if her next breath took too long to appear on her blanketed chest.

At almost 4:00 she started to moan and talk, so I got up and sat with her. She started with, "I've got to get up . . . I need to go to the bathroom . . . Let me up . . . Help me . . . Help me!"

She called me by name. I hated that I couldn't help her. I told her that her doctor had said she couldn't get up and that she could pee in her Big Girl Pants. She'd held it the last time for 16 hours, and it had been only about 6 hours.

"I need to go to the bathroom!"

That was her catch phrase for getting what she wanted when she wanted it. She wanted to walk but couldn't. She wanted to stand but couldn't. She couldn't swallow medications. She was so determined to try. A little sip of water was all she could manage. She was now fighting so hard to survive, to feel normal, to be . . . well, to be Barbara.

She fell back to sleep with a cold cloth on her head and one on her tummy. I took her air off, as she was pulling at it. It must have been causing some discomfort. Everything that I read said air does no good at end of life and causes more duress to some patients. But hospitals all want the air on and checked. Might be about dollars, or it might be perceived by some people that the medical staff didn't do enough.

Her hands were boiling hot. Her right leg was hot, her left one was cold. Both feet were hot. Her face was normal. Her tummy was doing some big time growling . . . that was new. The swelling in her legs, feet, and ankles had disappeared. There had been no need for diuretics for two days.

I guessed I was up for the day now. The day moaned on.

At 9:30 p.m. there was a knock on the door, and eight family members (whom I had seen but whose names I didn't remember) all arrived. Art, his mom, and Wanchai were with them. There were big smiles and chatter, and they were shocked then when they saw Barb passed out. Art went to her and took her hand. He said her name softly and touched her cheek. There was no response. She was not cognitive, as she had just had a big vomit and then morphine. They all got it.

Finally Wanchai said, "You tired, Rene?"

I said, "Yes, I'm ready to go to bed. It has been a tiring day for Barbara and me. We both need to sleep now."

He said something in Thai, and everyone said goodbye. Art's mom held my hand the whole time they were there. I really loved her and saw why Barb did too and why Art was the lovely young man he was. Wanchai was without question the love of Barb's life, and she was his. No wonder they both said, "Lucky, lucky us."

Once I was gone, everything would be Wanchai's job. He asked me to stay two more weeks, but I just said a flat-out no. Bob needed me, and I needed to go home. Wanchai understood, and he accepted my decision. My work was done. Almost. He wanted me to see the beautiful decorations that would be part of her funeral celebration.[1]

I was awake at 2:30 a.m., listening to Barb's noisy breathing and tummy racket as usual. I watched her sleep, concentrating on the rise and fall of the blanket across her chest, and finally dozed off until 6:30. Barb pooped around 5:00 a.m., I think. I didn't know until I went to wash her. I called for help. Two nurse assistants came and cleaned her, changed her, and changed the bedding. I suspected that this might be the lose-the-bowels thing at the end of life. Barb slept through it all.

When she woke up, she asked, "Did I have a stroke? What happened last night?"

By 11:00 a.m. there had been no catastrophes, and Art arrived. She was now stable. She had rallied again. Wanchai arrived and stayed all afternoon. He, Art, and Barbara chatted and had a lovely visit.

After they left, the doctor arrived, and I told him that she was usually vomiting three times a day. He wasn't concerned at all, as this was the norm in pancreatic cancer.

1   I had no idea just what this would entail. Not in my wildest dreams would I have thought what would actually be done at her celebration of life, which was five days long: a traditional Northern Thailand celebration, filled with rituals and involving the whole community. It would be amazing.

Barb's face was swollen (from water retention in her eyes, mouth, and lips), and she was given Lasix at 6:15 p.m. Big Girl Pants were working well, and I could clean and change her in no time at all. I had a system.

Barb was sitting on the edge of the bed after I had changed her, and I sat beside her. She said, "Rene, I don't understand what is happening to me."

I said, "Honey, you have pancreatic cancer. You know that."

"Oh, yes. I remember." She just leaned her head on my shoulder.

I held her hands, and I quietly wept.

There was a concert/buffet at the restaurant that night. The last time, 150 patrons attended, and Wanchai said they made some money from beer sales. Other funds went to the singing group as a fundraiser. I didn't know if Wanchai would be coming back to the hospital, as it would be a busy night for him, and he had visited with Barbara all afternoon.

It was a difficult time for us, and Barbara and I cried and grieved most of the evening. My heart was breaking as my sister was slowly dying.

Our night time unfolded: 9:00 p.m. meds and to sleep while I went to sleep at 10:00. At 11:00 Barb needed water. At 12:00 a.m. she needed a pee change and bedding change. At 1:00, Barb needed water. At 2:00, she needed morphine, and then she took all her clothes off. I sat with her. At 5:00, she vomited. At 8:00 she needed a pee change. Neither one of us slept much.

Art arrived in the morning, and he was just a love. He was calm, polite, and eager to please and do for us. We had a lovely visit as Barb slept, and then I sent him to Kad Suan Kaew to rustle up some lunch for the two of us. Wanchai arrived with some family members, and he washed Barbara's face over and over, very gently, as if memorizing every crease, every contour, every pore. He seemed to be bewildered and agitated, and I'm sure he felt totally helpless. He did not know what to do, but then neither did I.

He was still hell-bent on saving her life, and he bought into any promise of life after terminal cancer. We had done the monk in the mountain, and the latest was the doctor in the mountain. I felt so bad for him, as he was just so desperate. Like me, Wanchai was not sleeping well. He finally said to Barbara, "Why you make me love you, then you leave me!"

He took the girls for lunch at the hospital lunch place, but Art refused to go, staying with me and holding my hand beside me on the Chesterfield sofa. I don't think he wanted to listen to his dad talking about how he was going to take Barb somewhere and she would then get better.

When Wanchai came back, he had calmed down. We had a lovely conversation, and all was well. Art understood his dad. Most kids do.

The oncologist last saw Barb on Thursday, and he was shocked when he came in on Saturday. She had fluid in her lungs that was creeping up, and when he tapped on her liver, she cried out for the first time. We could lose her tonight, or she could still be vomiting and hacking a week from now.

She had lost any understanding of what was going on and was like a bewildered child. I just held her. She clung to me.

The staff took care of the diaper changes now, as they required two people. I just got warm water ready with soap and a cloth and I washed her.

Barb's eyes were better but still not good and might never be again. She said she could see all right, but who knew? When her pain doctor came this morning, he talked to her and to me. I said, "Is there anything you want to ask the doctor?"

True to form, our darling performed. She said, "Well, actually, is there any tasty food that I could have, something that has flavour? I'm so hungry and would like to have a decent meal." I wrote it down verbatim.

I didn't even let the doctor get to his usual "eat ice cream" suggestion. I just said, "Honey, your tummy is so fragile that all you can have is little sips of water. Anything else makes you throw up. I'm so sorry." The doctor just smiled and agreed.

She said, "Okay." The game was over.

Barb's vitals were still strong, except for oxygen levels. She was lucid. We had a little talk. There were some towels she wanted Art's mom to have, and I told her I had paid the bill up to yesterday. I had one week left before my breakout, and this would prove to be a very difficult week.

After the rough night with only two hours of sleep, I showered and went quickly to the store to pick up some breakfast while she slept. The pain doctor came in, and I told him about her difficult night. He said he would prescribe a sleep aid. He had given it before and stopped it because she was sleeping too much. I said, "Does that really matter, now, that she sleeps a lot?"

He said, after some thought, "No." I hoped that it would work, as we were both exhausted.

I ordered morphine for Barb. Her vitals were all stable. She just lay in bed, sitting up at times. She could not converse, but her heart was strong. Coughing last night was minimal, but there continued to be some yellowing in her eyes.

When I asked her if she was feeling really tired, she vehemently said, "NO, I'M NOT!" She was going to fight to the end in typical Barbara fashion. She had taken very good care of herself for many, many years, and so she had the strength to go on, long after others would have lost the battle.

Barbara was hallucinating all afternoon. She asked me to bring her table closer, and then she wrote a letter with her finger on the table. She said it was about how she had a big dog. Barb said, "I have to keep moving because if I don't move, the dog will die. It needs to move, and I need to do the same thing."

Then she said, "Moving will keep me alive. Eating will keep me alive." She had not eaten in weeks. She was still fighting the good fight.

Wanchai came for his evening visit after collections, and after he left, Barb told me that Wanchai didn't want her to take any more morphine, because that was what was killing her. This was so confusing for everyone, and we were all trying to find something that would keep her with us.

After he left, I went online and found the offending website. There was the "drink lime juice" cure and many others, with the advice to never take morphine under any circumstances. Morphine was the only thing that kept Barb from going insane with the pain. Cancer was not an easy disease — especially not this one.

Before going to sleep, Barb was answering questions that I hadn't asked. This day she showed the worst disorientation yet. She knew who I was, and I was part of her delusion. The straw in the glass became frightening to her until I took it out and showed it to her. She commented, "Oh, I'm daydreaming again."

Our time together this day had been sweet and gentle. The next day, Barb cranked her bed table up and down repeatedly, drummed her fingers on the table, or tapped her water glass over and over. She would lie down for half an hour and then be up again, sitting on the edge of the bed, arranging the items on her bed table in specific order, like everything in a row or in a circle.

Barbara was very thirsty, drinking lots of water, probably due to the diuretics. I'd had twelve hours of sleep in four days. Barb had not had much more.

She kept saying, "Rene, what am I going to do? I feel so awful. Can't they do something to make me feel better?"

I had no answers for her. I tried to console her, but she wanted miracles.

She had morphine at 10:00 and finally slept with a cold cloth on her forehead. I kept wet cloths in the freezer so that I always had a cold cloth available. The tap water was not cold. She took her oxygen off every chance she got, and I tried to be very gentle about putting it back on. It was nasal, and the nurses said they could get a mask. I said, "Do you think that she will keep a mask on when she won't keep the nasal tube on?" Her blood pressure was high again.

At 10:30 in the morning, Barb said, "I'm ready for this to be over. I think so. I am ready to be reborn now."

The doctors were trying to find medications that would allow her to sleep. The oncologist decided to do an ultrasound again to see whether he could remove liquid from her tummy area with a needle extraction to make her more comfortable. I went with her while she had the ultrasound, and the technician marked the area that showed liquid collection with a blue ink pen.

Once back in our room, the nurse said that they might put Barb on IV morphine instead of the breakthrough morphine, as she needed morphine every three to four hours.

Her doctor came in and Barb refused the needle extraction for now. He put her immediately on IV morphine instead, which doubled her dose. It just was not doing the job anymore, and she was always in pain. The body would get used to the morphine and then require a stronger amount. The cancer was spreading.

She cried in front of the doctor and said to him, "I'm not afraid to die. I know what is happening. I just can't stand the pain any longer. I want to go now." It was very telling. I had read about how patients finally get to the point where they're pain-free but basically comatose until they die. One week ago, the doctor could prod her belly without causing her discomfort, but now it hurt to be touched anywhere near the abdomen.

The morphine kicked in, and she was then in a blissful drug-influenced world, leading an orchestra or conducting a choir. If she stayed in this state, I would be happy. No pain.

Even if she were in a semi coma, her heart would thump on, as would her liver and kidneys and, so far, her lungs. She was not showing any sign of lung distress, even though they were slowly filling.

How many times had I thought or said that the end would be very soon, like a matter days? I took it all back. No one could really know. She had given up and was no longer fighting, but her body was really tough as nails — very skinny, bony nails.

We both slept a bit, and Wanchai called. I said not to come this evening, as Barb was finally asleep and I was going to go back to sleep as well. It had been a traumatic day.

Nights had been hell for my sister. Barb was up all night except for a couple of hours. I didn't think she would pass before I left. Her heart was way too strong. I would just have to trust that she would be in good hands. I continued to hope that she would lapse into a coma, as that would alleviate a lot of worry. Eventually she would probably succumb to congestive heart failure like our mom had, except Mom did not have cancer or its pain, and her journey was very swift and without the discomfort Barb had. This last week for me was the very worst. I wondered if this ache in my chest was now a permanent part of my physiology.

Barb wavered between total control, giving me good ideas as to what she wanted, and talking incoherently to imaginary people. Every day was different, sometimes every hour. She asked me to do a final clean off of her computer. Wanchai would take it over. I complied.

She talked now about dying and had accepted it as the final result, her goal being to do it pain-free, and Barb on a mission was formidable. We talked about her deciding to let it happen, as opposed to fighting death, and I think that she understood. Neither of us knew how to do that, but I did know that it would make a difference. She had told both her doctors that she was ready to die, that she was not afraid to die, and that she did not want any more pain. She and I finally talked about this, too. She was trying to take responsibility for her own death. She was so brave. When she was coherent, our talks were deep. We were both okay.

That night Wanchai felt better. We had a happy conversation after Barb went to sleep. He loved her so much it was scary, but he would survive. The good thing about this was that he'd already had an adjustment period without her at home. He and Steve were good long-time friends, so Steve would fill in a lot of the gaps. Wanchai had turned the two dogs into outside dogs, and he said, "Don't tell Bahbella! She know, she mean me!" *Mean* was Wanchai's way of saying "be angry." Those dogs were supposed to be inside pets, but the ticks got the better of him when Koke died of tick fever. *Soi* dogs seemed to be immune to them and were happier carousing about outdoors.

So I counted the days and the hours in the day, while I did as much as I could to make Barb more comfortable. I could even change her Big Girl Pants, wash her, and change the bedding by myself in 15 minutes. This was easier than calling for help, and I washed her better. We had long gotten over any embarrassment. Sometimes it took a while for staff to come and help, depending on their workload. They used tap water, which was cool, to wash her, while I heated it up by adding water from the hot pot so that it felt warm. Thais were a lot tougher than we were.

Chapter Thirteen

"Treat every moment as your last.
It is not preparation for something else."
—Shunryu Suzuki

WE woke up at 7:00 a.m. after a total of nine hours sleep. I felt like a new person. As soon as she was awake, Barb said she was in pain, and the nurse upped her pain IV morphine from ten to fifteen. Her pain doctor said he had put a sleep medication in the morphine to help her sleep. The oncologist came in, and Barb again said she didn't want the needle aspiration. He agreed that it was too invasive and he was better off using pain medication instead. Her pain now went all around her body, so he upped the drip to twenty.

Once again, a huge rainbow appeared, close to the hospital — a sign of Mom, we agreed — with a smaller rainbow behind. It was comforting to think that Mom might be nearby.

I had only four more days to watch Barb in agony. I could do it now. The light was at the end of the tunnel. She would still be with us but hopefully in a state of semi-consciousness and would not know I was gone. She remembered nothing from yesterday or an hour ago, and that was a blessing.

She could no longer make decisions and then made bad ones, like insisting that I put a large cold cloth on her belly on top of her pajama top; she got cold, and we had to get a nurse to change her wet top because she was attached to an IV pole.

This was now just a waiting game. After Saturday night, it would be out of my hands, and I had to let it go. Her pain doctor talked about keeping her sedated, but her oncologist liked to do procedures and keep her moving so pneumonia didn't set in.

The next day started at midnight, when I woke up to the sound of Barb rustling and found her at the foot of her bed, trying to walk. She had pulled her IV out, and the bed was wet with fluid. I called the nurse, who helped clean her up and then put in a new line. Barb was extremely agitated.

"Help me! Help me! Let's go! Now! Let's go! Help me!" Over and over, she cried out.

She continually stood up and then sat down on the bed and would not lie down. She played with the table, rearranging items, and continued to sit and stand. From where was this energy coming? At 8:00 a.m. she was still up and doing repetitive actions — obsessive, compulsive behavior. I was bagged again, but she seemed fresh as a daisy. The high morphine dose was the culprit.

The head nurse came in and said Barb's IV was shot, leaking badly. She called in our anesthesiologist, who was able to avoid a central line by finding another good vein.

When I told him he was magic, he smiled and said, "And so now I will disappear." Barb told him that she was ready to die and wanted him to just put her to sleep so she could sleep until it was over. He said he couldn't do that. He did give her a sedative to make her sleep. I needed one too, but no luck with that.

Barb was telling anyone who would listen that she was ready to die, like it was her next great adventure, and I guess it was.

There was something blue on two of her fingernails, and she spotted it and said, "Oh my God! It's happening!" I looked at it and rubbed some off. Somehow she had blue ink on two nails. I didn't know where it came from. Perhaps she had touched the blue marker they had put on her tummy for the ultrasound.

In the morning, Barb drank over 500 cc of water, so she had a huge pee at noon. After I changed and washed her, putting on new Big Girl Pants, she questioned me. "Where did you learn to do that?"

I just smiled and said, "Necessity, darling!"

She said, "I can't believe it. I'm a baby again!" We laughed together.

Suddenly she grabbed her bucket and put her fingers down her throat to make herself throw up. She said she had done that once before, as it made her feel better. It certainly worked. Barbara had always hated to throw up, but now she would do so just in order to feel better. It was all about perspective.

By 2:00 p.m. Barb was quite delirious. She had been sitting up on the bed edge for one and a half hours. "Why are all the black ping pong balls flying around on the floor?" The balls were the casters on the IV pole and her bed table.

"Let's do some things again," she said.

"Like what?"

"Let's throw up again."

"Maybe later."

"Let's go to lunch."

"We can't go out, but I can get you something if you want."

"No thanks."

The nurse came in, and Barb filled her bucket with all the items on her table. The nurse seemed puzzled and asked her what she was doing. Barb just smiled.

After the nurse left, Barb started biting her IV line. "Honey, if you put a hole in your line, you won't be able to get your medicine," I said. She stopped.

"Don't bite. Don't bite!" she said to herself.

Then she took some of her cream for her bedsores and began to smear it on her IV lines. When I asked her why she was doing that, she smiled at me and said, "To make you crazy."

She told me there was a man standing to her right with his back to us. "Do you know who it is?" I asked.

"No, it's a stranger, and I can't see his face. He's not scary."

Her pain doctor came in to check on her, and he upped her IV morphine a bit again.

Then she said to him, to me, and to the nurse, "I am afraid I might hurt my sister."

Her doctor said, "Why would you hurt her? You love her, don't you?"

"Yes, I love her, but I might hurt her. I said *might*. And the other people I might hurt are hiding in that closet." She pointed to the wardrobe.

Later she said there was a little boy with a hat on sitting on the bed. She fell asleep at 8:00 p.m.

At midnight, I was awakened by the sound of a horrific cough. Barb was choking and reaching out to me. I quickly got up, raised her upper body, and whacked her back. She gasped, clearing the blockage, and began breathing. I put her bed almost upright, with pillows behind her back for support and climbed in with her, holding her. She shook with whole-body tremors for almost one hour (the clock was in front of us on the wall). She finally fell asleep, waking up at 3:00 and at 5:00; she looked at me each time and then went back to sleep. I finally got out of her bed at 6:00, showered, and dressed. She stayed asleep, mouth open.

At 6:00, the staff took her vitals. Temperature and blood pressure were normal, but heart rate was 157. Her big toe was dark purple, her face cool to touch.

At 6:15, Barb said, "I need to pee."

I said, "Okay, honey, just go in your Big Girl Pants."

"Oh, I already went." She took her pajama bottoms off. They were dry. She removed all her clothes and managed to keep them off for about five minutes, but then she allowed me to put them back on. We had a new game.

She rearranged everything on the bedside table over and over, and she folded her comforter dozens of times. She wanted up, out, over there, over here, to drink water, to go to the bathroom, to walk down the hall. She whipped off her oxygen whenever the mood struck. So her waking times were a challenge. She was very, very active.

Morphine was at 25, Midazolam (for seizures and insomnia) was at 5 milligrams, and NSS (saline) was at 250 milliliters. Her feet were mottled purple, and her fingers and lips were blue. Barb was extremely agitated and wanted all her clothes off.

She asked me, "What happened last night when you lifted me up?" I told her she had been choking.

She became pensive and then said, "When are we going home?" That felt like a knife in my heart.

We had a talk about the fact that I was leaving on Sunday. She listened but didn't comment.

I was going to Doi Saket, to Barb's house, early on Sunday morning, and spending the day packing and doing chores from the list that Barb and I had worked out. A lot of it was paperwork. Some of it was distribution.

I suspected that Barb wouldn't know I was missing by then. She was on IV morphine plus the patch, a sedative, and a glucose drip. The sedative made her sleepy, and the morphine made her nuts.

She was obsessive and compulsive when awake, so I had my hands full. She tried to quickly get her clothes off before I could catch her. When I asked her why she was naked, she smiled at me and said, "I dunno!" She had her hospital top hanging from her arm, as she was attached to a pole, and her Big Girl Pants were around her ankles. I just had to laugh. This provided her with great amusement as well.

But her sleeping times were worse, as twice now she had choked while sleeping and hadn't been able to breathe. The first time was when I woke up to her gagging; I got to her in time. The second time was in the afternoon and I was close to her.

My biggest fear was preparing to leave her and having to listen to her begging me not to go, but I thought that perhaps that wouldn't be an issue. Her short-term memory wasn't good. She wasn't in any kind of pain. She saw people who weren't there, things that didn't exist. But the pain with pancreatic cancer is excruciating, so being nuts from the morphine was a good trade off.

My wish was that her lungs, which were filling with liquid, would just stop working or that her little heart, which was working overtime, would just stop beating. She was exhausted after a Big Girl Pants change, and that was only twice a day. Giving her Lasix, a diuretic, would mean seven or eight changes in a twelve-hour period. This was too much. She couldn't use the toilet, a catheter, or a bedpan.

So we struggled along here at Sriphat Hospital. I hated the thought of leaving her, but it was time. I needed to get back to my life, my husband, my animals, my friends, and my hobbies and grieve there. But I wouldn't have missed this experience for anything. You really find out just what kind of person you are, and you find out what love is all about.

Starting at 4:30 p.m. Barb dressed and undressed herself eighteen times, repetitively. Wanchai came at 7:00, and he managed to take her for a "walk." I left so they could have some time alone. During that time, she told him that I was "going away," so I know that she did remember today's talk.

Wanchai hired a man, Kow, to care for Barb at the hospital after I left. He had cared for Wanchai's mother and grandmother at their end of life.

He would stay here with her as I had been doing, and the nurses would do diaper changes and bird baths. Barb knew him and was happy with that arrangement. I felt then that I could go without feeling quite so guilty about leaving her alone. She couldn't be alone, ever. Period.

Another night was gone. Barb had been given a sedative and slept through until 5:30 a.m. She had disrobed twice by 6:00. I didn't care if she was naked. She liked to put her clothes back on, too.

After morning procedures, she went back to sleep so she could work on all the ways with which she was going to keep me spinning for the next two days.

When she woke up, I asked her who I was, and she just stared at me and smiled.

I said, "I'm your sister, Rene."

No change in expression. I hoped she stayed this way. She was pain-free and didn't know what was going on. I just didn't want her to suffer. After all she had been through, no more suffering, please.

I can't even imagine what would have happened to my sister had Sherry and I not been here. There was no way that Wanchai could have been there all day and all night for all this time, so Barb would have been alone for a lot of this. Often Thais die at home with their families around them. Barb wanted to go home, and Wanchai said maybe he should take her home, but the pain medications she was on wouldn't have been available at home, only in the hospital. The pain couldn't be controlled. So it had gone how it should have gone, except I would be leaving her. But she wouldn't know. I hoped.

I just needed to get through today and tomorrow, and then Sunday I would be busy packing and doing things for Barb. The plan was for me to take a tuk-tuk to Doi Saket at 10:00 on Sunday morning, and then Wanchai would take me to the airport that evening after his rent collections.

Barb's heart rate went up in one hour from 75 to 109, and she had been napping — no exertion. I was going to miss her passing by a very short time, I thought. This was going to be just awful for Wanchai when I left.

Barb and I talked about "permission" many times, and Barb knew that it was okay to let go, that she was well-loved, that during her crossing she would be "perfect," and that she would be reborn. We also talked about the fact that Mom and Dad were waiting for her.

She wanted to walk, and she sat on the edge of her bed, then stood, then sat, then stood. Repetitive actions. I took her out onto the balcony in her wheelchair, but just when we would get out the door, she wanted back in. It was exhausting for both of us. Maybe with me gone, she would let go. That might be what she was holding on to.

I paid her hospital bill up to that day and would leave Wanchai with some money for one more week. Anything after that, he would have to take it out of their joint account. Barb had set up her finances to take care of herself. She hoped that her savings would last, so as not to burden Wanchai financially too much. Wanchai called the payment tellers vampires, saying, "They just suck out all your money." But this was so inexpensive compared to Canada and U.S.

At 3:00 a.m. I was waiting for the nurse to put in a new IV line. An hour earlier, Barb managed to remove her diaper and rip out her IV line, so there was blood and morphine all over the bed. We usually got her pain doctor to do her lines with a local, as her veins were mostly collapsed now.

The nurse got a small line in, and we hoped it would last until morning. Barb usually had a sedative at 8:00 p.m., which knocked her out for the night, but it hadn't worked tonight.

She asked the nurse to help her get out of bed and go to the toilet. She couldn't walk. She was wearing Big Girl Pants. The poor little thing was so out of touch with reality. The worst thing was that she was awake. She took off her oxygen. Her oncologist was away until Sunday night, and he had been fighting to get a central line into her for a week; she'd rip that out too.

I feared that the upcoming days before she died were going to be just hell for everyone involved. But I just had tomorrow and tomorrow night. I could do that.

My Barbara had disappeared a while ago. She begged the doctors to put her to sleep until she died, and of course we can do that only to the animals we love, not to the humans we love. We could do neither in Thailand.

I didn't know what she was using for energy. She hadn't had a "meal" for three months, not even a sip of juice for over a week. She found it difficult to swallow water. And yet she carried on.

The doctors said that there was significant brain damage due to oxygen deprivation. Also, the cancer had migrated extensively to the brain. She knew she was going to be reborn. She wasn't afraid to die — at least, that's what she said over and over. I didn't know if this was usual, although I understand that this path was very personal to each individual. She'd had end-of-life symptoms for several weeks but none were strong enough to push her over the edge, and they keep coming and going. I wished that her countdown would be shorter than mine. I would be home soon, but where would she be?

At 6:00 a.m. Barb's blood pressure was back to normal, and her other readings were normal. When Barb woke up, she didn't know who I was, but she did say I needed to get rid of my awful lime green t-shirt.

I said, "That's my Phi Phi Island t-shirt. Remember when you and I bought t-shirts on Phi Phi Island?"

She thought for a moment, smiled, and then began to play an imaginary ukulele. She sang, "You and me, on Phi Phi."

I could see that her time was drawing closer. I hoped that I would never have to go on morphine. Damned if you do, damned if you don't!

Barb removed her Big Girl Pants, then her top. She sat naked for about 20 minutes. Nurses came in and wondered what was happening.

I simply said, "She likes to take her top off." They left. I doubt that this was new to them. Then Barb would put her top on and tie it up, and as soon as it was tied, she would untie it and take it off. Repetitive action.

Suddenly she said, "Let's go for lunch."

This time I just said, "Okay, I'll get ready," as I knew she would forget in a few minutes. She did.

I didn't think that Barb would die while I was there. Her colour was good, her vitals were good, and her heart was strong. Nothing was breaking down physically.

She had been sitting for a half an hour and was due to void soon, as she had gone twelve hours without voiding. Then she began her sit-stand regime. After almost an hour, she was exhausted, and she let me put Big Girl Pants on her. I put her to bed. I weighed Barb in the morning, and she had gained 40 pounds of water since we'd arrived. She hadn't eaten for weeks.

Wanchai came and brought me chicken-and-cabbage soup, which was so delicious. Barb was very quiet when Wanchai was there and didn't disrobe or pull her pants off. Barb got her sedative and went to sleep, and Wanchai and I talked. He really didn't know what to do with himself. "I no feel like that no other woman," he once told me. Tears filled his eyes. "How I live without her?" He fought so hard to get her, to keep her, and now he would lose her. I would go back to my life, but he was living his life. My heart ached for him.

As Barbara slept, I packed up my suitcase for Sunday and put it by the door, out of sight. I didn't want to pack in front of her. I left out my cosmetics and tomorrow's clothing.

Early in the morning, she had a pee, and I cleaned her up, including bedding. Then as soon as I crawled into bed, it was, "Water, pain, I need to throw up" (she didn't). I caught her putting her fingers down her throat to make herself vomit. The nurse came in and upped her pain medication.

She was sitting on the edge of the bed, snapping orders and complaining about her pain, and then she stood up and started pulling on her IV lines. She was meaner than a hornet, and every nasty characteristic that she had (and we all have a boatload of them) was out front and magnified. I didn't know how I was going to manage her. She should still have been sleeping. Her pain doctor was going to have to come up with a remedy for her agitation.

I knew this was about morphine and had been cautioned not to take things personally, so I was emotionally ready for anything she could throw. At least I thought I was.

She took her bed apart. She tore all the sheets off. How she managed to stand for these long periods was beyond me. And of course the two faces of morphine always appeared, as when a doctor showed up, she smiled and said, "I'm fine! Better than yesterday!"

When self-destructive behavior is a personal choice, it's sometimes easy to turn your back, but when it's medication driven, it tears at the heart.

Barb decided that she wouldn't do anything I asked, which was the opposite of how it had been all along. She tried to con the blood-pressure girl into taking her for a walk. Understand that she could only take two or three steps, but she could plant her feet and legs soundly (which now contained 20 pounds of water each) and looked very sturdy until she had to move. I was constantly worried about her falling and hitting her head.

She had rallied yet again! I feared that she was nearing her demise when she choked in bed, jerked, and quivered for an hour. I was so scared that night as I held her. I wasn't ready to let her go, but then, would I ever be? This was just so different, and I wasn't used to this new aggressive behavior.

The man who Wanchai had hired to take over when I left would have his hands full. Or perhaps not, as familiarity breeds contempt. She might do her best to please him. I also was sure that she was really angry with me for leaving, so this new aggression could have been payback on her part as well. Aren't we an interesting species?

She began undressing again. I just watched her do this. When the young water guy came in, he got a big shock but filled the water containers very quickly.

She pulled her IV out again, so now there was no way to deliver her medications. She was sitting stark naked on the side of the bed as the nurses tried to clean up the blood that was all over. This was quickly becoming more than I could handle. I just didn't know what to do. The nurses got a small line in and sedated her. I went to bed. But not for long.

Chapter Fourteen

"Nothing goes right on the outside
when nothing is going right on the inside."
—Matthieu Ricard

THIS would be my last day at the hospital. I would leave Sriphat one day early.

At 2:00 a.m., Barb woke up, took off her oxygen, and ripped off her IV again. There was blood everywhere. I called for a nurse, and we got her cleaned up. It took two tries to get a new IV in, around 3:00 a.m.

I tried to get her back to bed to go to sleep. She needed water. She needed to pee. She didn't want to put on a diaper. She wanted to go to the bathroom but couldn't walk. Her legs were hard as rock, filled with water. I finally convinced her to pee in her Big Girl Pants, which she did, and I changed her and the bedding. I went back to bed. Then we were up. She needed water. Pain, pee, water, pain!

"I want out," she said. "Help me. Pain. Help me, help me, help me!" Any pain I felt came nowhere near hers.

After her vitals were taken at 6:00 a.m., she took all her clothes off and tore out her latest IV line. The nurse didn't know what to do. She decided to wait until the doctor was available. For two hours Barbara was naked, not tied to an IV pole, moving furniture around the room. She had the strength of a lion. I just watched her. She seemed oblivious to my presence. I just wanted to keep her safe. If I spoke to her, she didn't answer. She didn't look at me; she looked through me.

Suddenly she said, "I'm calling the nurses." She reached for the call button, looked at it, and then threw it on the floor. I went over to her and picked it up to put it back, and she grabbed it out of my hand. I tried to take it away, but her grip was unbelievably strong.

She pushed the button over and over, and when it was answered, she screamed, "Help, help, help!" I backed off and went back to sit at the table, wondering what she would tell the nurse when she came. No one came. They were probably waiting for direction from me.

She put a hospital top on inside out (she had no IV now) and headed out the door. I asked her to stay in the room, but she ignored me. I didn't know how she was managing to walk. I followed her out, and she turned right, to a set of stairs, but the head maintenance guy stopped her and said that she had to go back to her room. She argued with him as I watched from our doorway. He called for two orderlies, and the three of them almost dragged her back into the room. After they brought her back, I stayed there by the table and watched to see what was going to happen next. I suggested going to bed to rest but was ignored.

Then she took her suitcase out of the cupboard and put it on the bed. I said, "Barb, what are you doing?"

She said, "I'm going to Doi Saket."

I replied, "Honey, we live here at the hospital now."

And then she lost it. "I'm going home!" she screamed. "You can't stop me! Nobody can stop me!"

When she'd started disrobing and doing other strange things, the doctor had told me two things were happening. First, the cancer had moved heavily into her brain, causing the loss of social boundaries. Second, the bizarre behavior, paranoia, and anger were side effects of the massive amounts of morphine she was taking. What a terrible Catch-22. She needed the morphine for the pain, but the trade-off was being totally nuts.

It absolutely broke my heart to see my darling sister reduced to this out-of-control person. I knew that I could no longer stay here. I was raw down to the bone. There was no recognition in her eyes, only the fear of a trapped animal. She was alone in her personal hell.

I was finally at the point where I had nothing left to give. I stayed at the table writing in my journal, stomach churning, waiting for time to pass so that I could call Wanchai, but I knew that he would probably sleep until 9:00 a.m.

She was pointing an outstretched finger at me as she just stood there naked, leaning on the bed table. She continued to scream loudly that she was going home, glaring at me without recognition. I was the enemy. I realized that I'd become the reason for her angst and therefore the target because I was leaving. My poor girl. She was no longer on IV morphine, so pain would be hitting hard soon.

Barb's phone had no more minutes on it, so I went to the nursing station and called Steve, asking him to ask Wanchai to come get me. When I returned with the nurse to check on Barb, she asked the nurse for a paper and pen, all the while staring at me, pointing a finger, and sticking her tongue out. I grabbed my things quickly, as I didn't want to upset her even more.

The nurse brought her paper and a pen, and Barb sat down on my bed to write. She kept glaring as I hovered in the doorway, stopping writing to shake her finger at me. She hadn't been able to sign to pay for her hospital bill for two weeks, but now she was writing a letter. She had been upright since 2:00 a.m., much of it on her feet, yet she hadn't been able to walk more than two or three steps for a very long time.

I waited outside after bringing my suitcase out and retrieving my cosmetics and one outfit from the closet while two nurses tried to calm her down. I didn't know just how out of it she was. I hovered in the hall, waiting for Steve and Wanchai. It was 8:30 a.m.

One of the nurses called the pain doctor, who needed to put in a new IV, and he told them to sedate her. Four nurses marched down the hall and stopped outside the door in conference. They went in and were able to give her the shot, perhaps telling her that it was for pain when it was really a sedative. I crept to the door so I could hear or see what was going on, and she was waving the piece of paper at them and screaming, *"Policia! Policia!"* They managed to get her into her bed and left her to wait for her doctor. I went back down the hall to the fountain area and sat on one of the leather couches.

I could hear Barbara hollering from the room. The nurses had propped the door open.

"Hellloooowww! Anybody! Helllooooww! I need some help here! Helloooowww!"

The nurses all ignored her, just walking past the door without looking in. They ignored me too. As long as she was hollering, I knew she was safe.

About 10:00 a.m., Steve arrived, rushing up to me. Wanchai was parking the truck. I was crying hard as I told him that Barbara was in really tough shape and that I could no longer handle her. Morphine exacerbates personality traits. For example, a suspicious and distrustful person would be extremely paranoid with high morphine dosages. This was one tough medicine. Barbara had snapped. Again, we thought the catalyst was the fact that I was leaving. Wanchai arrived and went in to see her immediately. Then Steve went in, and I asked him to try to get the paper to see what she had written. He couldn't get it from her but did see some scribbling on it.

While I waited, the pain doctor arrived with a nurse and put in a new IV line and gave Barbara another sedative.

Steve came out and said, "Oh Rene, she is so insane. She contradicts herself in the same sentence. She doesn't know where she is or what is happening." He went back in, and he and Wanchai went back and forth. Finally, Wanchai said that Steve would stay with her so she wouldn't be alone, and Wanchai would take me to Doi Saket. Then he would pick up the man who would stay with Barb.

I never thought I would actually say this, but I hoped she would die soon, and I feared she wouldn't. Dying without dignity was the cruelest blow. I didn't want this to be her legacy. Because it wasn't. It wasn't right that a human being who was loved and adored should have her personality ripped away, leaving her with an unrecognizable character.

We were all just reeling from that morning, and I just couldn't help her anymore. I left for the house with Wanchai at 1:00 p.m. and spent the rest of the day at Doi Saket, packing to go home to Vancouver Island. I planned to do the jobs tomorrow that I had promised Barb I would do.

Art arrived with his mom after visiting Barb, who had been calmed with sedation, and had his mom take him to a 7-Eleven to buy us chicken and sticky rice for dinner. His mom dropped him off, and Art and I microwaved our dinners and ate together.

Wanchai's sister Pum and one of her daughters came for a visit and to say goodbye to me. They had just come from the hospital. They all laughed about the fact that Barb had told them that her cozy comforter was made up of live chickens.

Barb hadn't known who her visitors were. Art said, "For eight years, she always call me 'honey' and give me hug and kiss. Today she look at me with strange eyes that had no Barbara in them. No 'honey,' no hug, no kiss. Like . . . no Art." Art and I had a long talk about all of this. He would be fine eventually. He and his aunt still laugh about the chicken comforter.

Art's mom came back to say goodbye to me. We talked for half an hour, even though she spoke no English and I spoke no Thai. Amazing. I genuinely loved these people. Art stayed in his room and watched television.

Barb owned a lot of pottery that Sherry had made and wanted some of it to be shared with the family: two bowls for Art, two bowls for Art's mom, and two bowls for Wanchai's sister. So they made their choices. All the rest of the pottery was to stay with Wanchai.

After they left, I went to bed at 9:00 p.m. and fell asleep quickly. I didn't hear Wanchai and Steve come home.

The roosters woke me up as usual, and I did get a decent although fragmented sleep. Better than in the hospital, for sure. Wanchai, Art, and Steve were still sleeping. Julie the bull was munching grass outside the bedroom window, a beautiful goodbye from the gorgeous creature whose enjoyment of fruit Barbara and I had shared on so many occasions. I loved Big Julie!

I went out into the carport and was greeted by Barbara's two dogs. Thunder had turned into the most delightful little, happy dog. He roamed free but stayed on the property, with lots of tail-wagging and no jumping up or biting. He had big, beautiful brown eyes. Dao, the old rescue dog, was now an outside dog too, and he and Thunder got along fine, trotting the property together. When Barbara had first gone to the hospital, Dao had pined for her, so Thunder replaced Barb in his life. Dao rested more, of course, and Wanchai tied them up at night together. So they were both *soi* dogs, as they were meant to be.

All the warning signs showed that Barbara was going to snap, and one day less would have left my heart intact. My distress wasn't for myself — I knew her behavior was all from the cancer and drugs — but my concern was her genuine fear that she was alone. She was surrounded by love, but she needed to know and accept that.

I hoped she didn't remember what had happened yesterday when she woke up today. She would often cry out, "Mom! Mom!" in her sleep. It felt like Barb was being tortured, and even though I held her and tried to soothe her when she awoke, I couldn't begin to parallel her anguish as she fought her way to understanding. She would get there. Would I?

I guess my toughest emotion was regret that I couldn't say goodbye to Barbara. *Goodbye* was not a word to be taken lightly. *Goodbye* was final. Not just "Farewell!" or "See you later!" Not "So long for now!" or "Take care!" I didn't say goodbye to her. Maybe that was meant to be, too. Maybe I should never say goodbye.

Chapter Fifteen

"No one saves us but ourselves.
No one can and no one may. We ourselves must walk the path."
—Gautama Buddha

SUNDAY morning, after I woke up to the crowing of the roosters and visited the dogs, I did some e-mailing, had a shower, sipped on a coffee in the swing, and walked around the property. It was a beautiful, warm, sunny day befitting a departure back to reality. I wandered through the yard as Barb had done in the early hours of her last morning here. I couldn't fathom how one looked at a loved home and gardens knowing this was the last time.

I decided to take some pictures of the gardens. Painting with acrylics was my hobby, and I loved to paint exotic flowers and, lately, portraits. I was starting to feel pretty beat up, but it was mostly emotional. Taking photographs redirected my thoughts for just a little while.

Wanchai went to the hospital at 10:00 in the morning, but before he left, he went to the market and brought me back a lovely omelet for breakfast and some vegetable soup for dinner. A friend came to visit Steve, so I retreated to the bedroom, alone with my thoughts. Would I ever be in this room again? Did I ever want to be in this room again?

Barb was everywhere in this house, and she had told me where everything had come from and the story behind it. She had chosen each item, each piece of furniture, always with Wanchai's approval, with thought and pride and love. And now she walked naked in a hospital room pushing a bed table and sticking her tongue out at imaginary people. Cancer. Drugs. Insanity.

By noon I had finished packing and went to the pool. The bowls had been distributed, and the special towels had gone to Art's mom; only the camera that Barb wanted Steve to have remained undelivered. Wanchai had put it away for safety. Some more friends arrived to visit while I was in the pool.

Finally it was time to do the last deed. I showered, got dressed, and went into Barbara and Wanchai's bedroom. It was time to clear out all of her personal possessions, as Barb had felt that Wanchai wouldn't be able to do this task.

I put all of her clothes from her wardrobe and drawers into plastic garbage bags and put them in my room. I also cleaned out most of the bathroom of her personal items, leaving only some things in the back of the cupboard under the sink. The bathroom items I put into a separate bag. I threw nothing out, just got everything out of the bedroom. Then I went back into the pool. It was lovely and relaxing to my body, but my mind was a tumultuous cesspool. I was tired, and there was no peace.

When Wanchai came home at 6:00 p.m., I showed him what I had done and assured him that nothing had gone into the garbage. I also had cleaned out Barb's personal files, taking what I would need in Canada, and I left all of Barbara's ESL teaching material and her books. Wanchai would have to dispose of these things as he saw fit. He wanted Barb's clothes to go to poor people.

Barb phoned Steve twice that day and asked, "What happened yesterday? Why is Rene gone? Is she all right? She was supposed to go to Doi Saket on Sunday, not Saturday."

Steve told her that nothing had happened, that I just had a lot to do and needed the time. It gave me some peace to know that she had no memory of Saturday. I alone had the job of erasing from memory the brain-damaged, drug-driven events.

Wanchai and I left for the airport at 8:30 p.m. and were there just before 9:00 p.m. It was so hard saying goodbye to him, especially after a tearful goodbye to Steve and Art. I did think that I would return one day and see them all again. We loaded my bags onto a cart, and Wanchai stood by the truck, which was parked beside the curb, waving, crying, and saying "I love you!" I was crying and saying, "I love you too!" It was so hard to leave him.

I hadn't been able to say goodbye to Barbara. I'd been afraid to go back to the hospital that evening, even though Wanchai had offered to take me.

I didn't know how I could leave her. This may have been a mistake, and it's a cross I have to bear. I just couldn't stand the thought of saying goodbye to her. I was a coward.

The last words I said to Barb when I tucked her in the night before that last day were, "I love you, honey," and her reply was "I love you, too." That was the last thing we said to each other every night when I put her to bed. I hoped that she remembered those words instead.

Several weeks before, Barb had asked me to please fly back first class so that I could sleep going home. She knew that I would be exhausted, which I was, and first class would mean that the two-night flights could be spent sleeping. That advice was her final gift to me.

One thing I realized after spending this time with my sister and being so closely involved with her journey was I lost the fear of dying that I had carried for so long. I was the elder sister. I should have died first. But that was not necessarily a truth. I realized it was such a waste of time and energy to worry, as life will happen as it should. Dying lost the scary connotation that had been my mindset for so long. I'd watched my sister moving along for months, with grace, ready for that final step. She was ready, but I was not. Barbara had become my teacher. I needed to become the student.

At the airport, I upgraded to first class, and we took off at 11:59 p.m. on Sunday, July 14. I sat in my first class window seat, and then it was Monday, July 15. I sipped my orange juice, and as we took off over Chiang Mai, I could pick out Sriphat Hospital, so close to the runway. I silently wept and now tried to say goodbye to my sister. She was there, then, but would be transferred to hospice on Tuesday and would leave us all on Thursday. Too soon, too soon.

The first thing that I did on the plane was to write a letter to Barbara, one that she would never read, but I hoped that she would still get my message. Here's what it said:

So, how are you now, my darling? How much longer can you push that little body? You rallied so many times when I thought I had lost you. But I know that the end is now close. Goodbye, my dear, dear sister. I love you so much and I hope that you know that with all your heart when you leave us. We talked so much, but how much do you remember? Are you dying in peace? Do you really know how loved you are?

Your life has been a turbulent one. Choices. But you were fearless in your adventures and moved on each time. Why did you find Wanchai? He loves you so, despite your frailties and you told me that with him you finally learned how to love unconditionally. That kind of love is known by so few and recognized by fewer. You always said "Lucky, lucky us." And you and Wanchai were meant to be together even though the time was short. You had so much against a future together, yet you overcame a multitude of roadblocks and continued to forge ahead, on to this new life not knowing that it would be sweet, but short.

Mom always loved you unconditionally and Wanchai and I learned to, as well. You were not easy to love, but you were worthy.

You opened up Thailand, Buddhism and the Thai culture to me, all of which I would not have known and you presented it all to Sherry too. You gave us your Thailand family who adore you and accept you as you are. They accept us too.

You were a difficult child, stubborn, challenging, always pushing the envelope. Mom said you were willful and lacked the perception of consequences, but without you, our lives would have been less and your grandchildren are the future. Life goes on through them. Mom and Dad just adored you and you know that.

I wish you to cross over in perfection and be reborn with a new understanding.

I could not say goodbye to you. How do you say goodbye forever?

We will all eventually be ok. We will never stop missing you, or wanting it to be different, as a world without you is so lacking, but we will be fine. Your journey is now just beginning and you have much to do. I know you will be watching us and smiling.

Forever, my sweet girl, your loving sister, Rene.

And then I slept.

Chapter Sixteen

"Don't cry because it is over.
Smile because it happened."
—Dr. Seuss

MANY hours later in Incheon Airport, as I waited for my final flight home, I e-mailed Steve and asked him to deliver a message to Barbara. I said, "Tell her I love her more than she can imagine and she will be forever in my heart. Every time I hug one of my family, I will be hugging her, too. We have been wonderful sisters, and I am so lucky I got her."

On Monday, July 15, Steve and Wanchai met with a panel of Barbara's doctors, and they all decided it was time for hospice care. This meant no further attempts medically to prolong life, only to make her remaining time as comfortable and pain-free as possible. This was end-of-life care. They went to visit McKean Hospital, which was a leper colony many years ago and now offered hospice care, especially to expats. It was typically not considered to be part of the Thai medical system, although Thais could use it.[2] Wanchai agreed that this would be best for Barbara, and they were shown a ground floor room overlooking gardens. Barbara's doctors had said that she could

---

2   Looking back, I think Barb should have been in hospice care her entire last week. The oncologist had told me that only hospital and home were available to patients. But he was referring to the Thai medical system, as hospice was available for foreigners outside the system; I hadn't known that. In Thailand, family does what might be considered hospice at home.

go on for another four or five weeks (in actuality, it would be three days), and she agreed to be moved to McKean Hospital.

When Steve and Wanchai arrived at Sriphat, Barb couldn't talk or open her eyes, but she held their hands, and when one of them would say something, she would squeeze tight. Steve talked about the fun things they had done over the years.

Steve thought she did not have much time left. She was not in pain.

Wanchai settled the final bill at Sriphat, and at about 3:00 p.m., they transferred her to an ambulance to take her to McKean. The transfer was smooth, and a hospital nurse went with them to fill in the staff at McKean.

Steve and Wanchai spent all day with Barb on Tuesday. She was calm and could understand them, so Steve gave her my message. She smiled and said, "That's nice." Steve also told her that Sherry had written a beautiful e-mail and that we both missed her and loved her. She understood him.

Wanchai spent all day Wednesday with Barbara, and on Thursday morning he knew this would be his last day with her. He was with her before 8:00 a.m. She was awake and said, "Wanchai!" when he got there. He got into bed with her, and they hugged. The head of nursing from Sriphat came to visit about noon. She brought beautiful pastel flowers in a tissue wrap. Barbara held the flowers and wouldn't let go. Later, when the orderly changed her diaper, she said, "Wanchai, I hurt." He told her he didn't want to see her hurt anymore.

That morning on the way to the hospital, Wanchai stopped at his bank and withdrew 80,000 baht (just under $3,000). He told Steve that Barbara was going to die that day. (The hospital staff may have advised him of this.) He brought all his gold jewellery as well.

During the day, Barbara hardly moved, but she would squeeze his hand when he spoke to her. Her eyes were mostly closed. At 3:00 p.m., Wanchai called Steve and told him to come to the hospital by tuk-tuk.

Wanchai did an old Thai custom. At 4:00 p.m., he laid the 80,000 baht all down her body, from her toes to her head and down her arms. He put bills in her hands and closed them. He laid his gold on her chest. Then he addressed her spirit, not her, in Thai. He said, "It is time now to leave this body. There is to be no more pain. You are to look after Eila (Mom), and I will watch over you here. You are rich now, so you can go. You need nothing."

Within a minute of this, Barbara took her last breath. She died elegantly. It was 4:30 p.m. on July 18, 2013.

Steve arrived ten minutes later, and Wanchai began to remove the gold and the money from her body. Steve took her hand, which was still toasty warm. He said she had never looked more beautiful. Her face was free of stress, her colour was good, and she looked completely relaxed. Wanchai stayed with her, stroking her hair, her arms, her hands, and face, speaking gently to her, for five hours.

Then he washed her body. The nurses warned him that sometimes fluids could release. This did not happen, and Wanchai said he was so proud of her. He dressed her in a white dress with pink underneath, her favourite colours to wear in Thailand.

In the morning, they notified the lawyer and the Canadian consulate.

After I received a loving e-mail from Steve to let me know of Barbara's passing, I made the necessary phone calls and wrote a letter to friends and family. It read as follows:

My dear sister Barbara has now completed her final journey. She left us yesterday at 4:30 p.m. Chiang Mai time, after many months of battling advanced pancreatic cancer. It was a peaceful crossing in the arms of her wonderful Wanchai, as it should have been.

For the last six weeks, I lived with her in Sriphat hospital, Chiang Mai, except for a six day hiatus, when we went back to her house in Doi Saket so that she could work on her bucket list. My daughter Sherry was with us for the first four weeks and we three laughed, cried, comforted and philosophized together.

Barbara's last two weeks were heavily morphine driven so that she was able to remain mostly pain free, but the side effects of this drug proved to be even more challenging than before. I called myself quick draw McBucket. I learned to be a bedside caregiver and the true meaning of unconditional love. I would not change one moment of my part in this life drama and am so grateful to my family who were so supportive and showed that they are made of "the right stuff". Thank you to them.

To Barb's wonderful friends who emailed, sent photos, told her stories and kept reminding her that she leaves a legacy of care behind her, I say, your actions were paramount in helping her endure this last four months.

When you see a rainbow, that is her, pointing to the pot of gold. When you feel a fresh breeze, that is her, soaring around you reminding you that life is good and meant to be enjoyed. When you feel the wonder of nature, that is her nudging you to not be afraid to step out of your comfort zone and truly live your life. She did.

Epilogue

"Peace is the highest bliss."
—Gautama Buddha

SHORTLY before the anniversary of Barbara's passing, Sherry and I returned to Chiang Mai, seeking some closure and some additional details regarding the missing days after I had left Barbara and before she died on July 18 of 2013. We stayed at Wanchai's resort in the *sala* (gazebo), which was filled with the essence of my sister, as it was her last project at her home before she became ill. Barbara, Wanchai, Bob, and I would have coffee on the deck of this *sala* most mornings when we holidayed with them, even though we stayed in the main house. It was a glorious, peaceful, serene place, with the small creek in front, filled with fish, which Wanchai lovingly fed each morning as we chatted and planned our day.

Now, it was Sherry, Wanchai, Steve, and I who had coffee (and fresh tropical fruit) each morning on the *sala* deck. It was during these morning visits that I was able to glean additional information from Steve regarding my missing days.

Returning to Doi Saket was like stepping back in time in many respects. The roosters woke us up just after 5:00 a.m., as before, and when Sherry opened the drapes, we spotted Julie the bull, grazing in the field next door.

Sherry found Barb's wide-brimmed bowl on one of the tables and filled it with water.

"What are you doing, honey?" I inquired.

"I am going to repeat Auntie Barb's tradition," she said. "We are going to have Leelawadee blossoms floating in this bowl, every day, while we are here." I had told her about how Wanchai had planted the trees and how they honored Barbara.

There were always fallen blossoms on the ground that looked perfect. So each day, we picked them up and floated them in the bowl, which was either on our table on the deck outside or inside beside our bed.

We were on a mission that first day. Sherry and I wanted to trace the steps of Barbara's last journey. After showering and dressing in cotton shirts and pants, we donned our wide-brimmed hats and left the *sala,* turning to the left at the end of the driveway. It was only about 80°F, as it was still early in the morning. As we passed familiar rice fields and country homes, I tried to visualize that same trip, taken almost eleven months before, while Sherry picked wildflowers.

When we arrived at the crematorium field, the gate was closed but fortunately not locked, although the open lock dangled on the fencing. Almost an hour passed by as we wandered the grounds and wall-less buildings. We sat on the turf in front of the tall, covered fire pit and cried. Sherry dropped the wildflowers into the pit, and after pulling the gate closed, we slowly walked back to the house to meet Wanchai. Sherry picked some delicate, white Leelawadee blossoms from Barb's yard to take with us on the next expedition.

On the road front, there were several long, narrow strips of land owned by family members. Wanchai and Barbara's home was built on one, and Wanchai owned the one next to it. The next strip was owned by Wanchai's cousin, who had inherited the land from their grandmother. She rented that land to rice farmers. In the center of this long strip of land was a large island of trees that rested on top of a buried ancient temple. This became sacred land, so the island part could not be cultivated and was very thick with foliage.

After a cremation in Thailand, the family usually gathered the bones that were left, filling a medium-sized bowl purchased specifically for this purpose. The bowl of bones was then buried or disposed of in whatever was the family tradition. (In America, after a cremation, the remaining bones are ground into ash so the family receives ashes only.) Wanchai gathered Barbara's bones, and they were buried on the island beside his family members. Barbara's share of our mom's ashes and a small representation of my dear friend Elizabeth's husband, John, were there as well. We had buried these ashes on a previous visit to Thailand. This island was very visible from the house — only about a five-minute walk away, across empty land and then through the rice field.

Wanchai came with us for this first visit and showed us the spot where Barbara's bones were buried. Sher placed the white Leelawadee blossoms on the ground. There were no markers, no headstones. Barb was beside Mom and John. Each of us said some words to the wonderful people who were represented here. Now I knew where Barbara was.

There were two spirit houses on the island, nestled amongst the heavy trees and vines, one very old and dilapidated and one newer, painted in bright colours. The new one had a recent offering of an opened bottle of pop resting on the platform, and Sherry placed a mango that she picked from a tree on the way onto the old spirit house, near our family. It was a good thing to feed the spirits.

A few days later, Sherry and I visited the island again, just the two of us, entering the rice field from the far side. We spent some time there, remembering and sharing our thoughts. I removed some earth to reveal bricks to show Sherry that this indeed was the ruins of an ancient temple.

Sherry decided that we should take the shortcut home across the recently cultivated rice field, which was very soggy, as it was rainy season. There were dry ridges to walk on, and against my protests, we managed to get near the fence, almost home. The last 20 feet were very soggy, but there were some boards on the ground. Sher began to make a walkway for us so that we could get to the fence opening and onto firm, dry land. She led the way. Almost halfway across, she missed a small jump and landed in a mud hole, sinking halfway up her calf. It was like quick-mud, holding her foot and leg tight.

I was trying hard not to laugh out loud. She was dressed in pristine white, her blond hair flowing, waving her arms about as the dark mud held her firm.

"Mom, I'm going to lose my Birkenstock!" That would be an expensive sandal to leave in a mud hole. Slowly she wiggled her leg and foot until the mud released her, with sandal intact, but now both feet and legs were covered in mud, almost to her knees. She sloshed her way over to the fence.

"Come on, Mom! Just walk on the boards!" Yes, I was going to repeat what I had just witnessed!

"I'm going back, Sherry, and I'm walking on the road. I'll see you at the house."

"Mom, there are lots of boards here, I'll put them down for you so you can get across to me." Slowly I made my way, board after board, until finally I, too, was out of the squishy rice field — without a mishap.

Then we realized that we had an audience. There were several Thais living in the houses at the back of the property, along this side road. They were watching from their yards. The children at play had stopped their games to take in the strange antics of the farangs. Even the dogs were staring at us.

"What do we do?" she whispered.

"Do what I do," I returned.

"Sawasdee-ka!" I said, giving my most respectful *wai*. Sherry repeated the gesture. The Thais all broke out into huge grins and returned the greeting. We had saved face and once again provided Thais with some entertainment.

After Barbara died last July, Wanchai had finally left to do the paperwork with the hospital, the lawyer, and the Canadian Embassy. The EMTs moved Barbara into her solid teak, gold-embellished casket and brought her home to Doi Saket. Her last request was finally granted. Steve was at the house, as was their Buddhist monk, Mitt, and all the monks from their temple.

The EMTs opened the casket, which was in the living room. Steve and the EMTs packed dry ice underneath and all around her. Then Mitt asked if she had a favourite blanket. Steve brought out her brown and white maple-leaf motif fleece blanket, which she had brought from Canada. We had used it in the hospital, sometimes covering her and sometimes me, depending on who needed the extra warmth because the hospital room was always air-conditioned for Barbara's comfort. Prior to that, the blanket lay on the back of the living room sofa. It was a cosy item, familiar to all.

Mitt placed the blanket over Barbara, tucked in the sides, and said, "Now Barbara won't get cold."

Then they sealed the casket and placed it in the corner of the living room next to the buffet. They surrounded it with flowers, and the five-day celebration of life began. That first night, the family slept on the floor in the living room so she would not be alone. During this time, the house and gardens were set up with one purpose in mind: to celebrate Barbara.

In the months before our mom passed away, Mom had had plenty of time to reveal her wishes regarding her own demise. She discussed these issues with Barbara as well, just to make sure that we understood the importance of her decisions. Her will stated that she was to be cremated. We talked about these things when we were at the art gallery doing our volunteer duties and there were no customers.

I asked if she wanted her ashes to be taken to Ontario and buried with our dad.

Her response was "Absolutely not! What a waste that would be!" I asked what she wanted us to do with her ashes. She said she had no special request. It was up to us. She followed up with, "And don't go spending money on a casket that is just going to be burned. Choose the least expensive one. I'd rather you girls have that money."

"And I don't want to travel to the crematorium in a hearse," she added.

"Why not, Mom?"

"All those strangers will be staring as we drive by. They will know I'm in there, and I just don't want strangers staring at me."

"But, Mom, you won't know."

"Yes, I will." Okay, no hearse. So she travelled in a discreet black van with dark windows, as Barbara and I followed behind in my car.

Mom also did not want any kind of ceremonies. There was to be no organized celebration of life, no funeral, no showing. "People will figure out what they want to do, if anything, on their own. I just don't want a big fuss." When Barbara and I were at the funeral home making arrangements, we asked if we could see our mom. Of course we could. They would "fix her up," but we said that wouldn't be necessary. We just wanted to spend some time with her before the cremation. The next day, we had to sign papers, and afterward we were brought into a nice room where Mom was on a table, wrapped in a white shroud. We felt her hands and her toes. It was our mom. Now we could let her go.

Mom had insisted that only her daughters come to the crematorium. She wanted absolutely no pomp.

Once there, Barb said, "Do you want to say something?"

"No, she knew we loved her. You can say something."

"No, it's okay." Then Barbara and I together pushed the button. We sat in the car for a while and then went and had a very nice lunch in a very nice restaurant and talked about our mom and how much we would miss her.

Barbara and I respectfully followed our mother's wishes. Mom was a quiet, reserved, private person, and her passing on depicted that.

Now, Barbara, on the other hand, wanted the full Traditional Northern Thailand Cremation Ceremony. She had attended many Thai funerals in her years in Chiang Mai, and she wrote e-mails to me giving great details of her experiences attending family services; this was before she was diagnosed. She did not discuss her own funeral with Sherry and me. That was Wanchai's territory.

For Barbara's celebration, Wanchai arranged for dozens of tables and hundreds of chairs to be delivered from the temple, and large tent tops were erected to protect people from the sun or from rain. The tents were at the side of the house and the back. Villagers came with food either prepared or cooked on the premises. Coffee, tea, water, and juices were delivered. Huge pots of soup simmered on portable propane stoves. Food and drink was available for all, all day and all night. Wanchai arranged for breakfast, lunch, dinner, and snacks to always be available for whoever came. And they came in the hundreds. The village women took turns cooking. This was a traditional celebration of life.

In the evenings, the monks arrived and musicians entertained playing Lanna music, which was the traditional music of Northern Thailand. People came and went, sometimes several times a day. People visited, laughed, remembered. Steve said he was shocked at the regular talk that started with "I remember when Barbara . . ." This was spoken in Thai, of course, but he understood, being bilingual.

On the second day home, the "house" arrived, in parts to begin with. It was 18 feet high once assembled, embellished in pink and gold. This was to be Barb's home until her cremation. It was utterly beautiful with its carvings and wispy pink fabric streamers.

Some of the village women weaved a very long white rope, and this rope was tied to the casket and used as a guide to bring the casket out of the house to its new home. It was all about connection. In a special ceremony, monks and family members carried the sealed teak vessel where Barbara lay to her house on the front driveway. It was placed inside the house, still very visible, and then flower arrangements were put all around her and on the ground. The housing and the casket with her enlarged photograph were very visible from the road, as was the custom. There were flowers, her photograph, and places to burn incense in various locations about the property.

For the next three days, it was just about Barbara and her life, her Thai family, her friends, her neighbors, her villagers. It was a celebration. At one point, a table was set up under a covering, and nurses were taking people's blood pressure. This was an opportunity for healthcare workers to offer this service to a large gathering of people.

On the fifth day, the family and villagers (over 400 in number) and Barbara began her last journey. Her pink and gold house, which represented a Buddhist temple, and her casket were resting on a big trailer. The monks attached the white rope for them to use, and other ropes were attached for the family and close friends to use.

Two people carried her photograph at the front of the procession, followed by the monks holding the white rope attached to Barbara's casket and housing. Family and close friends pulled on the ropes to move the trailer, first down the driveway and then down the road. The others followed behind, most with umbrellas overhead to protect from the beating sun. A truck with the live band was last, playing music, so the village could hear. Some men carried big sticks to push up the wires that crossed over the road every so often, allowing the tall building to pass beneath. There was lots of shouting in Thai when the top got caught on the wires, which happened often. The procession moved from her home in Doi Saket to the crematorium, about a mile away. This took about one hour in the 100°F heat.

The men pulled the trailer close to where the monks sat. They said some small chants, and then she was pulled to the site of the cremation.

The attendees each selected a paper flower/stick of incense made by the village women, which they blessed on their foreheads and then placed on a tray to be added to her casket building. A live band was playing Lanna music.

Family and helpers lifted the casket from under the gold housing and placed it on the crematorium platform. The family stood around the casket: Wanchai near the top, then his sister, Pum, then Steve. Monks, including Art, who became a monk for Barbara's crossing, were on the other side. They opened the casket to perform the final blessings.

Steve said that Barbara was looking directly into Wanchai's eyes. There was no deterioration or colour change of her body. She was perfect.

They anointed her with holy water, resealed the casket, and lowered it into the pit. The gold housing was then place on top of her. The firecrackers were lit and the rockets and fireworks went off, simulating the sound of elephants crying, which dominated the next few minutes. This sound comes from rotating rockets forcing air through slits of bamboo. Her spirit was shot up into the heavens.

If you search for "Traditional Northern Thai Cremation Ceremony," you'll find a YouTube video of her sendoff. It shows her beautiful gold and pink housing and its size. Yes, this video is of her.

Afterword

"True love is born from understanding."
—Gautama Buddha

TAKING this walk with my sister was just so surreal. I was grateful that my situation was such that I was able to do this for her and for me. My family was so supportive, and I was grateful for them. As author Stephen Levine wrote, "When you meet the pain of another with fear, it is often called pity . . . When love touches the pain of another, it is called compassion."

Our time at the hospital was so loving. Other than a couple of times when she became angry and I (or Sherry) walked away, the time we spent together was happy. There was more laughter than tears — the tears would come later. I was changed forever, and I knew that Barb was so grateful for our presence and our help and love. It was all right.

I came to understand that for me, there's no such thing as closure. There's only learning to live in a new reality. The cost of loving deeply is great, but only in loving deeply did my own existence make sense. Loving deeply involves vulnerability, which is a scary thing for a lot of people — "I don't want to get hurt!" But along with the pain of loss came such inexplicable joy and peace.

Sherry shifted in her own thoughts of life and mortality. She now feels that she can live life more fully, treat others more kindly, and exercise more patience. She has a better understanding of the finality of not just life but relationships, and she feels more prepared to allow the future to unfold as it should and would. She better understands impermanence.

We both were amazed at the human spirit's ability to do what is necessary in the face of great challenge. You can do it; you just do it.

Barb didn't deteriorate physically quickly. There was a lot of rebounding and maintaining. But her mental state moved like an avalanche, from bowing her head to Sherry in a *wai* to screaming at the top of her lungs to no one. So much changed in three weeks. She went down fast after Sherry left; I think she was really holding on for Sher's sake. Barb didn't cry much after Sherry's departure. I didn't know it then, but Sherry had said goodbye for both of us.

I have struggled with the fact that I promised her I would stay "until it was finished" but left before Barbara passed over. I broke my promise. I try to never break promises. For a few short months, we laughed, cried, slept, worried, and dreamed together. But I broke my promise to her.

I will continue to struggle with this. However, I do think that she was able to finally let go because I was gone. The shift was quick and strong after I left, and I would like to think that my leaving shortened the pain-riddled time my sister had left. It was right that Barbara's last few days were with Wanchai. They were together for the beginning and then for the end. I was the one who filled in some of the middle of her last journey with support of my beautiful Sherry and from the rest of our families.

On that final Friday night when my last words to Barb were, as usual, "I love you, honey" and she replied, as usual, "I love you, too," that was how we left each other, as the next day Barbara was no longer my Barbara. I stayed one week too long for me and one week too short for her.

Steve told me that he and Wanchai knew that she died having understood. "She understood: She got it. It was a peaceful crossing." And I believe him.

The account of the six weeks spent in Chiang Mai with my sister, Barbara Gail Lahti Stopanski, living in Sriphat Hospital for the most part, was compiled from my daily journals and from e-mails written to family and friends at home. It tells the story of my sister's battle with invasive pancreatic cancer and is what I saw, felt, and recorded: my observations and my opinions. It is her final journey through my eyes. It is about trying to say goodbye.